Union Public Library
1980 Morris Avenue
Union, N.J. 07083

P9-DZX-873

Salsas
of the World

Salsas
of the World

MARK MILLER

WITH ROBERT QUINTANA

PHOTOGRAPHS BY JON EDWARDS

Union Public Library
1980 Morris Avenue
Union, N.J. 07083

GIBBS SMITH
TO ENRICH AND INSPIRE HUMANKIND

First Edition
15 14 13 12 11 5 4 3 2 1

Text © 2011 Mark Miller and Robert Quintana
Photographs © 2011 Jon Edwards

All rights reserved. No part of this book may be reproduced by any means whatsoever without written permission from the publisher, except brief portions quoted for purpose of review.

Published by
Gibbs Smith
P.O. Box 667
Layton, Utah 84041

1.800.835.4993 orders
www.gibbs-smith.com

Designed by Ron Stucki
Printed and bound in Hong Kong

Gibbs Smith books are printed on paper produced from sustainable PEFC-certified forest/controlled wood source. Learn more at www.pefc.org.

Library of Congress Cataloging-in-Publication Data

Miller, Mark Charles, 1949-
Salsas of the world / Mark Miller with Robert Quintana ; photographs by Jon Edwards—1st ed.
p. cm.
ISBN 978-1-4236-2208-6
1. Salsas (Cooking) 2. Cookbooks. I. Quintana, Robert. II. Title.
TX819.S29M545 2011
641.8'14—dc22

2011008741I

Contents

Introduction

I have been in love with the idea of salsas my whole life, as long as I can remember. I love the idea of adding something more to my food to make it tastier, more interesting, spicier, more colorful. To give food more edible textures and make it more fun to eat has always seemed like a great idea. More flavors were better at four years old and they are still better today. "More is better!" was and is one of my great slogans in the restaurants. I believe that we should strive for more meaningful, more interesting, and more creative experiences in food and in life. And when it comes to food, what is better than something that you add to make it taste better! Salsas can make food more pleasing. And when food becomes pleasing—not just a nutritional necessity—it becomes a joy. You find out that food can make you happy!

The idea of playing with my food and creating new flavors at an early age wasn't always encouraged—or seen as the necessary developmental steps of a great chef—but I was given a large amount of latitude because I had an insatiable curiosity about food and why it tasted like it did. I would pop lots of things in my mouth as a way of learning about it. It's what we all do at early levels of learning, but I have never stopped.

At the beginning of our food experiences, we play with food when it gets put on our plate. We maybe feel like we are supposed to eat it because it makes our mother happy. But sometimes we don't eat it—because it's green, or it's bitter, or it's too strong, or it's too hot, or a hundred other reasons. The problem is it becomes an all or nothing approach to food. The main reason we don't eat certain food is that it is not what we like or want *at the time*. This can be hard to express when we are very young, and this problem can last our entire lives—sometimes people just don't know what it is they want to eat.

However, later in life, your big culinary breakout usually comes about when you get to choose what you like to eat. And you get really excited about food because now the possibilities of what you like just got a whole lot bigger. When you are a little older, you still don't go shopping and prep and cook all your own food, but you get to add ingredients to your dishes to make the food more what you like. So the food begins to reflect you and your tastes. You take more ownership in the process of creating flavors and foods that you are passionate about.

I remember from when I was very young that eating out was so exciting, not because I was going to a fancy restaurant or because it was good food, but because I got to order something that I wanted to eat. I got to choose. And I could spice it up to how I wanted to before I ate it. You can choose many different ways to build a hot fudge sundae—all vanilla ice cream one time; all coffee ice cream the next time; or with one scoop of coffee, one scoop of chocolate, and one scoop of vanilla the next time. You can use thick hot fudge and lots of whipped cream and leave the nuts off (which I discovered through trial and error interfered with the consistency and taste, and which I learned the scientific reasons for later on). A grilled hot dog was good, but a grilled hot dog with sweet honey mustard and homemade red-and-green piccalilli from my grandmother's pantry was a great hot dog, a memorable hot dog, one worth repeating, one worth looking forward to. We all have done that in our early eating lives: by trial and error created those flavors that are most satisfying. The trick is to keep creating them your whole life.

The lesson that I was learning early on was that good food became better when there was more to it. Another flavor added to the experience. I was becoming a flavor thrill seeker, developing a lifelong bent to seek out new flavors and new food experiences. I remember fried summer Ipswich clams from the Cape were wonderful, but the same yummy clams dipped into a creamy, tart, and sweet tartar sauce were fantastic! This was one of my first salsa experiences. Another was recognizing slices of roasted pork loin were tastier and sweeter with a homemade cinnamon-maple applesauce. The pork tasted better and the applesauce tasted more interesting when you ate them together. I was learning quickly that I liked my food experiences to have more flavors, more excitement, more mystery, and more fun than the normal kid. When it came to food, why be satisfied with less?

So my early culinary education started, and the more I created my own flavors the more interested I became in food, not just cooking it but eating it. I started in earnest to look for combinations of flavors that worked and tried to figure out the internal culinary flavor logic of each dish. I started with simple combinations: warm, velvety oatmeal with sweet maple syrup and rich, cold cream; peanut butter and jelly sandwiches; bologna with mustard; tuna fish salad with celery. I eventually moved on to more complex combinations: Maine lobsters cooked in seaweed with drawn butter; Polish sausages with sauerkraut; Italian sandwiches with meat, sautéed sweet peppers and onions, and melted cheese. My first foray into the world of food outside of the familial was pastrami sandwiches on rye bread with kosher dill pickles on the side. I eventually moved on to beef tacos, then Indian curries, then Chinese chop suey. My culinary world was getting wider and the combinations of flavors that worked together to create these memories were also getting wider.

Later when I went to university at Berkeley (where I studied Art and Culture in the Anthropology department), I started to cook for myself full-time. I was further exposed to the rich ethnic food traditions of the Bay Area. I started to learn more about intricate, more complex flavor combinations and I started to incorporate those lessons into my cooking. My food experiences and my academic studies were complementary: they were both teaching me about how different cultures expressed themselves in varied ways and that there was no " better" or "higher" culture, but that almost every culture had created masterpieces of the human experience in some form or another. And when it came to cooking, I learned that each culture has some great food! There is certainly no monopoly of great tastes and great food from just one particular cuisine.

Part of what I learned during those years was that because I was limited in funds, I had to make my food taste fascinating without buying expensive prime cuts of meat or gourmet products. I learned to use spices and seasonings to make the difference, and learned that the mastery of flavors was the key to a rich food experience. The world of salsas became important to my success, as they could create a number of delicious bites in the same meal. Simple, inexpensive Indian samosas became magical with a tamarind chutney and fresh cilantro mint raita; a grilled skirt steak was scrumptious with salsa fresca; and vegetable couscous with the addition of harissa and a few Moroccan merguz sausages was as satisfying, and even more so, that many richly ornamented dishes from classic European cuisines—and a lot more affordable.

When I cooked, the more salsas there were in the meal, the more interactive and fun it was for everyone. Salsas were a way that everyone could customize their food to their own taste and style, just like I had done as a kid. When you add a salsa to your food, you are actively taking part in the final taste. Your food becomes more personalized, more intimate, and more satisfying.

During the ensuing years while I was studying anthropology, traveling, and sampling the food of a diverse number of cultures, I came to realize that every culture has its own versions of salsas. I saw salsas pop up in tropical, magical Bali—a hot, herbaceous salsa of sweet soy and chiles served with suckling pig or Balinese roast duck. In Burma, I tasted strong, bitter, spicy salsas made from fermented tea leaves. These went on top of the baked tofu custards. At the storied city of Pagan, I sampled twenty varied salsas on the falafel carts of Jerusalem, outside the Old Wall. I added harissa to my wild boar couscous in the Middle Atlas Mountains of Morocco; I added pesto to my summer soup in Provence; I ate piquant peanut salsa on grilled beef heart brochettes outside of Cuzco, and discovered a myriad of salsas in market kitchens, loncherias, taco carts, and restaurants across Central America while visiting the majestic pre-Columbian ruins. Salsas were for breakfast, lunch, and dinner. They were part of the experience of eating that made it exciting, with endless flavor possibilities.

When I started my first restaurant, Fourth Street Grill in Berkeley, it was a casual restaurant specializing in fresh grilled fish and meats with lots of ethnic accents. Salsas were an important part of our food philosophy at Fourth Street Grill. We bought great ingredients, cooked them simply (mostly on the live mesquite grill), and created a range of flavor possibilities by altering the salsas. It was a perfect way to keep the food simply cooked. We had a small staff of three, including myself, for prep and cooking and had to serve up to 250 people per night without altering our operational efficiency and control of the process. We made salsas full of exciting flavors, and we made a lot of different salsas every day: they went on the fresh grilled fish, steaks, chicken, double-cut pork chops, and Provencal loin lamb chops.

From Fourth Street Grill to my next restaurant, Santa Fe Bar and Grill, to my third restaurant, Coyote Café, salsas became an even more important part of the menu. Food at my restaurants was centered on the great ethnic food traditions that I had discovered and enjoyed my whole life and that I find so full of passion and mystery. From Latin to North African to Asian, I was cooking food that was simple and honest in preparation—over a grill or from a wood-burning oven—but was complex, mutilayered, and rich in levels of sensory experience. Great ethnic cuisine depends upon the mastery of subtle techniques that have evolved for multiple generations in a culture over hundreds of years, executed at the highest level. They do not depend upon exotic, costly, rare ingredients or faddish ideas. My audience supported my culinary choices and I had a great career, with thirteen restaurants total on three continents over thirty years. I am very grateful to all my loyal guests who followed me across the culinary globe.

This book is homage to all the great cooks, whether they are cooking at home or in simple carts or market stalls, wherever they are, who serve great, honest food with wholesome ingredients and some wonderful bowls of salsa on the table. The recipes include my personally chosen favorite salsas from all over the world, from the very simple to amazingly complex puzzles of flavor combinations.

Salsas are used worldwide to customize and add accents and dimensions to snacks, soups, sandwiches, main plates, and roasts of meat and fish. As accessories of the flavor world, they dress up the meal and make it sexy. They give it bling! Salsas make food come alive on the palate by changing each bite with a different tempo, a different rhythm, and a different counterpoint. How long would you listen to a concert that had the same music (no matter how good it was) over and over again? The same thing holds true for food—the senses want something that keeps their attention by ever changing, endlessly creating new possibilities of experience.

Salsas are very healthy, as almost all are based on fruits and vegetables and herbs and spices, with very little extra fats or excess salts. They are easy to prepare and much more economical than buying prepackaged and processed salsas, which are usually pasteurized so the flavors have become muddled together and not spate and bright as a salsa should be. You can make a salsa very easily from scratch or one that starts from prepared ingredients that you can just add to or "dress up," such as canned black beans or canned fire-roasted tomatoes. These can be converted to a salsa in minutes.

My early food experiences and my early experiences with salsas shaped my own culinary philosophy, which is that by adding flavors and spices to food you can create an infinite possibility of personal pleasurable experiences, and that each culture has many different ways of creating delectable dishes. You can learn these possibilities and share them with others through your cooking and recipes.

I hope this book and these salsa recipes will enrich and add to the enjoyment in your gastronomic life and those you share it with, as they have mine. We spend a great deal of time in life eating, and thinking about and preparing food, so we might as well get the most enjoyment out of it rather than looking at it as a chore. Remember, at the end of the day the one who has the most fun wins! And what better way to have fun with your food than to "play with it," as I have done my whole life. Best wishes that you may find many new friends to add to your culinary world, friends that make you happy, that make your life more pleasurable and more interesting, and that are a joy to be with—as all good friends! To make something that tastes wonderful and to share that wonder and passion with others is to give a little more joy to life.

1 | Easygoing Salsas

Artichoke Fennel Provençal / FRANCE

I have thrown the whole Provençal garden and market into this one. It is really worth the trouble and has a spectacular finished look. It's easy to make; it just looks like a lot of ingredients but they all work together easily. Make some simple dishes around this recipe and the dinner is done! I make Artichoke Fennel Provençal and serve it as a first course with chilled rose wine, fresh goat cheese, and some wonderful black olive country bread with a rich Provençal olive oil. The use of fresh lavender makes the recipe very authentic. Use all the light, fresh fennel fronds from the plant—they are a great addition. If you can't find baby artichokes, you can use the heart of large globe artichokes; there will be a lot more waste but you will still have the same great flavors.

Juice of 1/2 lemon
24 baby artichokes
1 shallot
4 cloves garlic
1 tablespoon olive oil
1/2 teaspoon whole black peppercorns
1/2 teaspoon whole coriander seeds
1 bay leaf
1 bunch thyme
2 lavender flower buds
1/2 teaspoon salt
3/4 cup rose wine
1/2 cup thinly sliced fennel
2 tablespoons fennel fronds
1/2 cup diced red bell pepper (1/3 inch dice)
12 Lucques olives, pitted, cut in half
2 tablespoons olive oil
2 tablespoons rose wine
1 teaspoon finely chopped basil
1 teaspoon finely chopped tarragon
1 teaspoon finely chopped marjoram
1 teaspoon finely chopped thyme
1 teaspoon finely chopped chervil
1 teaspoon finely chopped parsley
2 teaspoons lavender flowers, picked

Prepare a bowl of water and add the lemon juice. Cut off the top of an artichoke and pull away the green leaves. Cut on a diagonal around the heart, then cut in quarters and place in lemon water to prevent discoloration. Repeat with the remaining artichokes.

Dice the shallot and peel the garlic; add to a sauté pan that has a lid. Add the olive oil, peppercorns, coriander, bay leaf, thyme, lavender, and salt. Heat the aromatics on low heat for 2 minutes. Add the drained artichokes and rose wine. Cover with a lid and let artichokes steam for 10 minutes.

Continued on next page

Remove the lid and let liquid reduce until dry. Remove the bay leaf, thyme, lavender flowers, and peppercorns. Place artichokes in a mixing bowl.

In a pot of salted boiling water, blanch the fennel and fennel fronds. Add to the bowl of artichokes along with the red bell pepper. Pit the olives and add to bowl. Add olive oil, rose wine, chopped herbs, and lavender flowers and mix gently. Yield 3 cups.

Serves 6
Heat level: 1 2 3 4 5 6 7 8 9 10

Tip: *It's all about the olive oil here. Make sure to use a rich, buttery olive oil from Provence or Spain; many of the Italian Tuscan olive oils are a little bitter for this dish.*

Shiso Leaf Tomato / JAPAN

My passion for Japanese food began when I started to cook and eat a lot of it in my university days at Berkeley. I had a Japanese roommate and was studying the culture of Japan and Chinese painting at the time. The cuisine—like the culture—has hundreds of layers. You learn one, only to find that there is another one beneath it. This salsa is definitely a fusion of flavors that I like and not an authentic Japanese dish, but it uses authentic Japanese ingredients throughout, and my Japanese friends like it. Try it with grilled Chicken Yakitori on the side, cold oysters, or over rice.

2 cups cherry tomatoes
3 tablespoons julienned shiso leaf (about 10 leaves)
1/2 teaspoon yuzo kosho paste, green (Yakami Orchard brand)
1 teaspoon organic soy (Kikkoman brand)
1 teaspoon sesame seeds, toasted
1/8 teaspoon Meyer lemon zest
1 teaspoon thinly sliced green onion, green part only

Slice the tomatoes in rings and place in a mixing bowl. Add the shiso leaf, yuzo kosho paste, soy, toasted sesame seeds, lemon zest, and green onion. Mix well. Yield 2 cups.

Serves 6
Heat level: 1 2 3 4 5 6 7 8 9 10

Tip: *The organic Kikkoman soy sauce in the black bottle is readily available. It really is a superior product. Make sure to get it; it costs very little for a soy sauce that does make a big difference.*

Green Chile Pistachio Pesto / NEW MEXICO

Not only does New Mexico have the best green chiles in the world but it also grows lots of fine pistachios, though most people don't think of New Mexico as pistachio country. And New Mexico also produces the only red chile– and green chile–flavored pistachios that I know of. I have found them to be great for gifts when I visit Japan—they go over big as a spicy accompaniment for drinks! The cured lemons in this recipe are the whole cured lemons that you can find at olive bars or in jars at Middle Eastern grocery stores. They are very easy to make at home (see page 188). I usually have a jar of cured lemons ready to go in the fridge, as they are perfect to add to salad dressings, pastas, butter, or oils. Make sure the pistachios are bright green inside the skin, a true Kelly green, and not dried out. You want pistachios from a new crop.

2 cups canola oil
1 cup pureed poblano chiles
1 1/2 cups cilantro leaves, no stems
3/4 cup green chile pistachios (Whole Foods bulk)
5 tablespoons lemon oil (Agrumato brand)
1 teaspoon cured lemon (about 1/4 lemon, sliced) (see page 188)
3 tablespoons olive oil
3/4 teaspoon salt
1 tablespoon lime juice

In a deep-sided pan, heat the canola oil to 350 degrees F and oil roast the poblano chiles for 3 minutes or until the skins blister. A splatter screen is recommended. Place the chiles in a plastic bag to steam. Peel and deseed when cool. Place the poblanos in a food processor. Add cilantro, green chile pistachios, lemon oil, cured lemon, olive oil, salt, and lime juice. Pulse to a fine paste. Yield 2 cups.

Serves 8
Heat level: **1 2 3 4** 5 6 7 8 9 10

Tip: *Try to find Meyer lemons when you are making cured lemons. They have a more penetrating, complex perfume than Persian lemons.*

Red Bell Pepper Espelette Salsa / FRANCE

A Mediterranean mélange of big Spanish flavors, this recipe showcases the specialist chile powder Espelette that is popular in the Basque country in Spain and in France. Many high-end restaurants started to use it a few years ago and it has caught on. Espelette is not smoky like pimento, and is richer and brighter than paprika. It is not as hot as New Mexico red chile power and has its own unique profile, which is very complex and not overbearing. Espelette is grown in Californian now. Make sure you are purchasing real Espelette by buying it from a trusted vendor such as The Spanish Table or Kalustyan's. The old-fashioned Pernod gives this recipe a splash of anise flavor; oranges and black olives are a natural together. This salsa has great colors, bright tastes, and the zing of the Espelette.

2 cups canola oil
1 1/3 cups red bell pepper strips (about 3 peppers)
1 1/2 teaspoons Piment d'Espelette, toasted
1/2 cup black olives, oil cured, pitted, and cut in rings (French Beldi)
4 teaspoons Pernod
1/2 teaspoon Microplaned orange zest
1 tablespoon orange juice
1 clove garlic, sliced on truffle cutter
1/4 teaspoon salt
2 tablespoons olive oil
3 tablespoons large chiffonade basil

In a 12-inch-wide x 4-inch-deep pan, heat the oil to 350 degrees F. Fry the bell peppers on all sides until the skin is blistered and the flesh is darkened. Carefully remove peppers to a plastic bag and let steam. When cool, peel, deseed, remove any white veins, and cut into strips, about 1- x 1/8-inches. Place in a mixing bowl.

In a nonstick sauté pan over medium-low heat, toast the Piment d'Espelette and add to the peppers. Slice the olives in rings and add. Add the Pernod, orange zest, orange juice, shaved garlic, salt, olive oil, and basil. Yield 2 cups.

Serves 4
Heat level: **1 2** 3 4 5 6 7 8 9 10

Ranchero Salsa / MEXICO

This is the tricolored salsa that you see on most Mexican breakfasts, on top of Sunny Side Up eggs with refried beans on the side and some warm, fresh corn tortillas. You can add more or less of your favorite chiles, and you can use vegetable oil if you like, although the recipe is named after a ranch where they have lots of hearty cooked foods. Do not let the salsa cook too long as you want to keep the individual items layered in texture and flavor. Most ranchero salsas have been sitting on the stove for hours and taste nothing like the simple, fresh version it should be. To make it easier in the morning to assemble breakfast, I usually fry the chiles a day ahead and have them peeled, but individually stored. The reason I use frying in this recipe is that the fire-roasted method is too smoky for eggs and not fresh enough. The fire-roasted tomatoes provide enough smoky, earthy notes. Ranchero Salsa is also good on fried chicken breasts, pork chops, or grilled fish.

1 cup canola oil
2 poblano chiles
4 serrano chiles
3 Fresno chiles
1 1/2 cups fire roasted and pureed Early Girl tomatoes
1/2 onion, sliced in strips
1 clove garlic, crushed
2 tablespoons lard or duck fat
1 teaspoon salt
1/2 bunch cilantro, wrapped in cheesecloth and tied
1 1/2 cups V8 Spicy Hot tomato juice

Heat the canola oil to 350 degrees F and fry the poblanos, serranos, and Fresnos in a skillet for 2 minutes to blister the skins. When cool enough to handle, peel, deseed, and cut in 1/8- x 1 1/2-inch strips; reserve. Fire roast the tomatoes and puree in a food processor; reserve 1 1/2 cups. Sauté the onion and garlic in lard or duck fat, being careful not to brown. Add the salt, wrapped cilantro, V8 juice, tomato puree, poblanos, and serranos and cook for 10 minutes. Remove the cilantro. When cool, add the Fresnos. Yield 3 cups.

Serves 6
Heat level: **1 2 3 4 5 6 7 8** 9 10

Late Summer White Corn and Hatch Green Chile Salsa / NEW MEXICO

This is a great late summer salsa for the BBQ table—a sort of Southwest succotash. Whether it is a side dish for other recipes in a night of grilling or just as it is on its own, you can use this salsa for everything from a side salsa to stuffing chile rellenos or even enchiladas. Corn and green chiles have an amazing affinity for each other; the sweetness of the corn combines well with the piquant, smoky chiles. Here I have included fresh, grilled nopales to make it even more of a native dish. The texture of the nopales, which some people find a little slimy, I think adds some textural interest to the recipe and the different colors complement each other. I like the contrast of the white corn against the blackened, fire-roasted chiles. I always like to use fresh basil with corn, as they bring out the natural sweetness and perfume of each other. Fresh marjoram adds another fresh, herbaceous note. This salsa is amazing with grilled chicken. Or try it as a vegetarian taco topping with a little crema or grated Cotija cheese on top.

3/4 cup chopped Hatch green chile
1 1/2 cups white corn
1/2 cup chopped nopales cactus
1 cup cherry tomatoes
1/2 teaspoon salt
1/8 teaspoon smoked salt
1/4 teaspoon sugar
2 tablespoons finely julienned basil
1 teaspoon finely minced marjoram
2 teaspoons olive oil
1 tablespoon lime juice

Over an open flame, roast the green chile and place in a plastic bag to steam. When cool, peel, deseed, and chop in 3/8-inch pieces. Reserve. Heat a cast iron pan or comal to medium-high. Roast the corn in a single layer. Do not move the corn; it should pop. This will take 1 to 1 1/2 minutes. Let cool; reserve.

Clean the cactus of any needles by cutting in the reverse direction they are growing. Grill over a medium flame and chop in 3/8-inch pieces. Let cool; reserve. Slice the cherry tomatoes in rings and place in a mixing bowl. Sprinkle with salt, smoked salt, and sugar. Add the basil to the tomatoes. Add the marjoram, green chile, corn, cactus, olive oil, and lime juice. Yield 4 cups.

Serves 8
Heat level: **1 2 3 4** 5 6 7 8 9 10

Tip: *Try to use fresh marjoram when available, as fresh oregano is a little too oily for some of the dishes. Marjoram is more subtle and sweeter.*

Fire-Roasted Tomato Piñon / NEW MEXICO

Try this easy, fast salsa that combines some very authentic Southwest ingredients, including the piñon nut and the tepin chile. The piñon nut has a rich, resiny flavor, and is prized as a special ingredient from China to Italy. Piñons are hard to extract from their hard shells from within the pinecones of the pinon tree. These nuts were a major staple of the Indian of the Southwest who gathered them. The piñon nut is nutritious, having one of the highest amino acid contents of any nut. The nuts were traditionally eaten in the fall and were used in food. Some Native Americans even ground the piñon nuts into a nut flour for a type of native bread made on hot rocks. This made a type of flatbread called piki bread. Tepin chiles are a wild chile that grows on the deserts of the Southwest. It's tiny—about the size of a pea—and fiery. If you can't find tepin chiles, you can use another small, hot chile like the Arbol.

About 18 ounces tomatoes (Early Girl)
About 1/2 small white onion
4 cloves garlic
2 teaspoons toasted and ground tepin chiles
1 1/2 teaspoons sun-dried tomato paste
1 teaspoon smoked salt
1/2 teaspoon salt
4 tablespoons whole piñon

Over a flame with a grill, fire roast the tomatoes, charring the skins. In a cast iron pan or comal over medium-low heat, roast the onion and garlic for 12 minutes. Toast the tepin chiles for 1 minute then crush. Place the tomatoes, onion, garlic, tepin, sun-dried tomato paste, smoked salt, and salt in a food processor. Pulse for 2 minutes. Stir in the piñon. Yield 2 1/2 cups.

Serves 6
Heat level: **1 2 3 4 5** 6 7 8 9 10

Tip: *Try to buy piñon nuts in the bulk section where you can taste the freshness. Many of the bagged nuts are old and rancid and can ruin your whole recipe. Always taste any nut or oil before adding to a recipe because at least 50 percent of the time, those products are rancid in the stores or in homes where they have been stored too long or at too high of temperatures.*

Rio Grande Corn and Black Bean Salsa / MEXICALI

I have been making black bean and corn salsas my whole life as a chef. When I opened Coyote Café in 1986 and started to cook exclusively with Southwest ingredients and techniques, we made about a dozen versions of black bean salsa—some even had tequila in them. And when we started our salsa line, Coyote Cocina, we of course made black bean corn salsa in jars. It was a hit, just like the fresh versions we had been serving for years. To make this recipe easy for you, you can use canned beans as I do in this recipe. They have a good consistency for salsas and make putting this together quick and easy.

1 clove garlic
2 cups corn (about 2 ears)
1/2 cup cherry tomatoes
1/2 cup diced red bell pepper
2 teaspoons corn oil, divided
1/4 teaspoon salt
1/2 cup diced poblano chiles
1/4 teaspoon smoked salt
1 cup black beans, drained and rinsed (Bush's brand)
1 chipotle en adobo, seeded, minced fine (La Costeña brand)
1/2 teaspoon Chipotle Tabasco

In a cast iron pan or comal over medium-low heat, roast the garlic for 15 minutes then mash and put into a mixing bowl. Increase the heat to medium-high and roast the corn in a single layer. Do not move the corn. The corn must pop. (This will take about 1 to 1 1/2 minutes.) Add the corn to the mixing bowl. Put the cherry tomatoes in the cast iron pan and blacken for 8–10 minutes. With the back of a knife, mash and puree. Add to the mixing bowl.

Deseed and dice the red bell pepper in 1/4-inch pieces and sauté in 1 teaspoon of corn oil for 3–5 minutes. Season with 1/4 teaspoon of salt. Add to the mixing bowl. Deseed and dice the poblano in 1/4-inch pieces and sauté in 1 teaspoon of corn oil. Season with 1/4 teaspoon smoked salt. Add to the mixing bowl. Add the beans, chipotle, and Chipotle Tabasco.

Serves 8
Heat level: **1 2 3 4** 5 6 7 8 9 10

Tip: *When dry roasting corn, get the pan hot first and use a heavy, nonstick pan for best results. Do not crowd the corn or it will not get caramelized; it will just steam.*

Mountain Yam Shitake / JAPAN

Delectable sweet potatoes are grown throughout Japan, and you see them especially in the fall during the street food festivals and temple celebrations, where sometimes there are more than 300 different food vendors in Kyoto. Even into late spring, during the cherry blossom festival viewing, there are trucks that come in from the countryside selling wonderful sweet roasted yams that are cooked in special wood and charcoal ovens fitted onto the backs of the trucks. Another famous street yam preparation is to cut them in thick wedges, making sweet potato fries that are then dusted with sugar and seven spice or Shichimi. The shitake mushrooms in this recipe are dark and earthy—woody against the sweet orange color of the yams—and the sansho or Japanese pepper gives it a mild peppery flavor. Be careful of the sesame oil that you use fresh sesame oil. Use just enough to suggest some richness, but do not overpower the mushroom and yams.

2 cups diced sweet potato
1 tablespoon canola oil
1/4 teaspoon salt
1/2 teaspoon sansho chile powder
1/2 teaspoon Shichimi (Seven Spice Powder)
1 teaspoon sesame oil
4 cups diced shitake mushrooms
1 clove garlic, sliced
2 tablespoons canola oil
4 teaspoons organic soy sauce
1 tablespoon mirin
2 tablespoons water
1 tablespoon lime juice
1/2 teaspoon ground dashi
1 tablespoon sesame seeds, toasted

Preheat oven to 375 degrees F. Peel and cube the sweet potato in 1/4-inch pieces. Place in a mixing bowl. Add the canola oil, salt, sansho chile powder, Shichimi, and sesame oil. Spread out in a single layer on a sheet pan lined with parchment paper. Use a spatula to get all the spices out of the bowl. Bake for 25 minutes. Let cool.

Prepare the shitakes by removing the woody stems and cubing mushrooms in 1/4-inch dice; reserve. In a nonstick sauté pan, place the garlic and oil and slowly start to cook the garlic over medium-low heat. When the garlic has browned, add the shitakes and cook for 4 minutes over medium heat. Add the soy, mirin, and water. Cook until the liquid has evaporated; remove from heat and cool. When cool add the lime juice. Mix in the baked sweet potatoes, dashi, and sesame seeds. Yield 2 1/2 cups.

Serves 6
Heat level: **1 2 3 4** 5 6 7 8 9 10

Chinese Chives, Sesame, Tomato / HONG KONG

This colorful, modern, Asian salsa uses Chinese chives; they have a more pronounced garlic flavor than regular small green chives. Chinese chives are much larger—they are the long, thin, flat green shoots from a bulb of garlic. There are two types of Chinese chives: the long green ones, which are younger, and the flowering ones with a closed bud at the end, which are more mature and a yellowish green color. Look for Chinese chives in Asian grocery stores. They make a nice accent for pan-fried dumplings or for Asian noodle dishes to freshen the taste away from the ubiquitous soy and oily sauces. They are also wonderful on grilled swordfish and added to other steamed fish dishes.

2 cups cherry tomatoes
3 tablespoons very finely sliced Chinese chives
1 teaspoon rice wine vinegar (Marukan)
1 tablespoon sambal oelek chile sauce
1/4 teaspoon sugar
1/4 teaspoon salt
1 1/2 teaspoons Hoisin sauce (Lee Kum Kee brand)
2 teaspoons sesame seeds, toasted

Slice tomatoes in rings and place in a mixing bowl. Add the chives. Add the rice wine vinegar, sambal oelek chile sauce, sugar, salt, Hoisin sauce, and toasted sesame seeds. Yield 2 cups.

Serves 6
Heat level: **1 2 3 4 5** 6 7 8 9 10

2 | Complex Puzzles Salsas

Apricot Aleppo / TURKEY, SYRIA

Robert made this fantastic, complex salsa from fresh apricots from a Santa Fe garden using his expertise in Middle Eastern flavors. It is a salsa fit for a banquet for an Ottoman prince! The flavors are a tapestry of Middle Eastern delights—golden, fragrant apricots perfumed with vanilla, honey, and saffron threads. It has an earthy, slightly smoky flavor from the Aleppo chiles and mysterious emerald bits of pistachios. We served it at our own Turkish feast, inspired by my amazing culinary journey through Turkey with a friend, Anissa Helou. Anissa is a stylish expert on all things Middle Eastern and leads small, exclusive culinary tours a few times a year. She also has many wonderful cookbooks and a very informative blog. Look at her website at ah@anissas.com for more information. Use this salsa with a grilled leg of lamb marinated with pomegranate molasses and sumac. Cooked on a wood-burning spit, the result is incomparable.

2 pounds apricots, pitted
2 tablespoons hot water
1 teaspoon saffron threads
1/2 teaspoon cinnamon
1 tablespoon Aleppo powder
2 tablespoons honey
1/2 ounce dried Aleppo chiles (about 8)*
1/4 cup dried unsulfured apricots
1/8 cup orange juice
3 tablespoons pistachios
1/8 teaspoon salt

Preheat oven to 200 degrees F. Cut the apricots in quarters and place in a bowl; set aside. In a small mixing bowl, put the hot water and saffron together and let steep for 1 minute. Add the cinnamon, Aleppo powder, and honey. Pour mixture over cut apricots and spread out on a half sheet pan covered with nonstick Silpat. Bake for 2 hours or until dried.

Deseed and stem the whole Aleppo chiles, then mince fine. If using a red bell pepper, cut out the veins and deseed. Dice the pepper in 1/8-inch squares, place on a sheet pan with a Silpat, and dry in the oven at 200 degrees F for 1 hour or until dried.

Dice the dried unsulfured apricots in 1/8-inch pieces. Place in a bowl, pour in the orange juice, and let soften. Rough chop the pistachios and set aside. In a large bowl, put the saffron dried apricots and add the dried apricots with orange juice, minced Aleppo chiles (or dried bell pepper), pistachios, and salt. Yield 3 cups.

Serves 8
Heat level: **1 2 3** 4 5 6 7 8 9 10

**You can use an oven-dried red bell pepper in place of the Aleppo chiles.*

XO / CHINA

This is a new addition to the pantheon of Chinese salsas. It was invented commercially in Hong Kong in the 1980s by the family that started the famous Lee Kum Kee brand of Chinese soy sauces. There are many versions of this salsa in other regions of China, but the Hong Kong version is the most famous and widely accepted. It is also the most expensive and complex of all the Chinese jarred salsas. The primary ingredient here is dried scallops, which are available from Chinese specialty herb shops and dried seafood shops in Chinatowns in larger cities. Or you can make your own dried scallops as we did here. The salsa has a dark, intense shellfish soy essence that enhances seafood and vegetable dishes in the best restaurants in the Hong Kong region.

DRIED SCALLOPS*

1 cup water
1 teaspoon salt
4 ounces fresh bay scallops

Place the water in a bowl. Add the salt and then the scallops. Put in the refrigerator for 4 hours. In a dehydrator set to 105 degrees F, dry the scallops for 24 hours.

SALSA

2 ounces dried scallops
2 ounces dried shrimp
2 ounces Chinese sausage, bacon, or dried ham (Serrano)
1/2 cup grapeseed oil
1/2 cup thinly sliced shallot
1/2 cup thinly sliced garlic chips (about 20 cloves)
1/4 cup grapeseed oil
2 cloves garlic, minced
2 tablespoons minced shallot
2 tablespoons finely diced fresh or candied ginger
1 tablespoon dried crushed Arbol chile
1 tablespoon sliced Bird's Eye chile (about 3 or 4 rings)
1 tablespoon oyster sauce
2/3 cup sherry wine
1 teaspoon palm sugar
1/2 teaspoon salt

**You can buy dried scallops at an Asian market if you prefer.*

Shred the dried scallops and dried shrimp in a food mill and steam for 20 minutes in a bamboo steamer set over simmering water. Fine dice the sausage and steam at the same time as the scallops and shrimp.

In a wok, heat the 1/2 cup oil to 325 degrees F and fry the sliced shallots slowly until golden brown. Remove and reserve. Fry the sliced garlic in the same manner, stirring often. Remove and reserve. Add the 1/4 cup oil to the wok and cook the minced garlic, minced shallot, ginger, Arbol chile, and Bird's Eye chile slowly for 5 minutes until translucent. Add the steamed sausage and cook for an additional 5 minutes. Add the steamed scallops and shrimp, oyster sauce, sherry, palm sugar, and salt and reduce until the liquid has evaporated and the wok begins to sizzle. Stir in the fried shallots and garlic chips. Yield 2 1/2 cups.

Serves 10

Heat level: **1 2 3 4 5 6 7** 8 9 10

Chimichurri / ARGENTINA

This salsa is probably derived from the salsa verde of Italy. It also has a Spanish accent from its first settlers—you can taste it in the use of sherry vinegar. Argentina had huge waves of Italian immigrants in the nineteenth century, and even though they had little wealth they brought their recipes and made an industry out of winemaking. The trick of really good chimichurri is not to get it too spicy; the herbs should be first and foremost and the spiciness in the background. Chimichurri is the absolute perfect accompaniment to magnificent grilled Argentine free-range grass-fed beef.

3 cloves garlic, minced
5 tablespoons minced shallot
1 teaspoon salt
1/3 cup red wine vinegar
2 tablespoons rice wine vinegar (Marukan brand)
1 tablespoon sherry vinegar (La Bodega brand)
1/2 cup Spanish olive oil
1 teaspoon Chile Caribe flakes
1 1/2 teaspoons black peppercorns, ground medium
1 fresh bay leaf, vein removed
3 tablespoons fresh oregano
6 tablespoons Italian parsley*
1/4 teaspoon rosemary
3 tablespoons fine sliced chives

Place the garlic and shallot in a bowl. Add the salt, red wine vinegar, rice wine vinegar, sherry vinegar, and olive oil. Toast the Chile Caribe and black pepper over medium-low heat in a nonstick sauté pan and add to the garlic and shallot mixture while still hot. Mince the herbs separately and combine with the garlic and shallot mixture. Mix well. Yield 2 cups.

Serves 8
Heat level: **1 2** 3 4 5 6 7 8 9 10

Tip: *Use a combination of fresh herbs and dried spices for a more interesting balance. If you use all dried herbs, the chimichurri will lack the freshness to accent the beef.*

**Use Italian or flat-leaf parsley for this recipe. It has a softer, fuller green note than curly-leaf parsley.*

Seoul Taco / KOREA

Seoul Taco—the Korean taco concept—took off a few years ago like wildfire, sweeping the whole country as the hot culinary trend of the moment. Invented in Los Angeles by the accomplished chef Roy Choi on his Korean taco truck, it's a great example of how the new American palate is made up of diverse culinary cultures that are compellingly fusing together diverse flavors and ingredients to create new dishes.

1 clove garlic
1/2 teaspoon smoked salt
2 teaspoons rice wine vinegar (Marukan brand)
4 teaspoons mirin
2 tablespoons maple syrup
3 tablespoons apple juice concentrate (Apple Time)
3 tablespoons Korean red pepper paste
3 tablespoons ketchup
2 tablespoons BBQ sauce (Hunt's hickory brand)
1 chipotle chile en adobo, seeded (La Costeña brand)
1 tablespoon Chipotle Tabasco
1 tablespoon organic soy sauce
1 teaspoon lite soy sauce
1 teaspoon sweet soy sauce
1/2 teaspoon black pepper
2 teaspoons sesame oil
1/2 teaspoon hickory liquid smoke

Crush the garlic and salt to make a paste. Place in a blender and add the vinegar, mirin, maple syrup, apple juice concentrate, red pepper paste, ketchup, BBQ sauce, chipotle chile, Tabasco, soy, lite soy, sweet soy, black pepper, sesame oil, and liquid smoke. Puree. Yield 2 cups.

Serves 8

Heat level: **1 2 3 4 5 6 7 8** 9 10

Salsa Verde / ITALY

At my first restaurant, Fourth Street Grill in Berkeley, which opened in the late 70s, we made this salsa by the gallon every day, fresh from scratch. The salsa was the perfect accent, in color and flavor, to our simple mesquite-grilled entrees. It was so popular that we had literally thousands of requests for the recipe, as well as requests to purchase it for takeout. You may be tempted to use a food processor for this, but it's much better done by hand using a large, sharp chef's knife. The texture will be better and the juices of the herbs will be more contained in the herbs themselves, so the flavors are more distinct and separate, not running together in a mushy and wet mixture. Traditionally, salsa verde was used in Italy as a topping for osso buco. You can also try it with tuna salad or grilled cheese panini, or on pizzas as a fresh highlight.

3 cloves garlic
1/2 teaspoon salt
1 1/2 cups olive oil
5 tablespoons fine chopped flat-leaf parsley
2 tablespoons fine julienned basil
2 tablespoons fine sliced chives
1 tablespoon fine chopped fennel fronds
2 tablespoons fine chopped tarragon
1/4 cup capers in white balsamic, minced fine
1/4 cup capers in white balsamic, rough chopped
6 lemons zested with a Microplane
2 tablespoons lemon juice

Using the tip of a chef's knife or in a pestle and mortar, mash the garlic with the salt to make a paste. Add the olive oil. Chop the herbs separately and add to the garlic and olive oil. Add the minced capers. Then add the rough chopped capers. Add the lemon zest and juice and mix well. Yield 2 cups.

Serves 6
Heat level: 1 2 3 4 5 6 7 8 9 10

Tip: *As soon as you chop the herbs, make sure to put them in the oil as they will darken if left exposed to the air too long. Salsa verde is best served within one day of preparing.*

Spicy Peanut / PERU

This salsa is a fusion of my two most memorable peanut salsas: one from the Andes and one from Southeast Asia. Peanuts were first cultivated in the high mountainous valleys of the Andes by the Pre-Columbian civilizations going back as far as 5,000 BC. The peanut was so valued as a crop that it was used as a symbol of wealth. We have many existing examples of hollow peanuts made of pure gold fashioned into huge necklaces for the nobility and royalty. Southeast Asia also has a great history of peanut salsas. All the satay street vendors of Thailand, Singapore, Penang, and Bali have their favorite versions to serve with small bite-sized grilled chicken and pork satays cooked over smoky, live charcoal. The Southeast Asian recipes use coconut milk and hot chiles along with sweet palm or date palm sugar.

4 cups aji panka chiles*
3 cups water
1 teaspoon white vinegar (Heinz brand)
1/2 cup diced onion
1 tablespoon peanut oil
1 1/2 cups dry roasted peanuts
1/2 cup peanut oil
1 tablespoon Habanero Tabasco
3 tablespoons Smokehouse almonds
3 cloves garlic
1 1/2 teaspoons salt
2 teaspoons brown sugar
1/2 chipotle chile, seeded
1 1/2 teaspoons organic soy
1/4 teaspoon black pepper

In a cast iron pan or comal, toast the aji panka chiles. Place in a medium saucepan and add the water and vinegar. Cook for 10 minutes, covered.

In a sauté pan, fry the onion slowly in the 1 tablespoon peanut oil. In a blender, place the aji panka with cooking liquid and sautéed onions and blend. Add the peanuts, 1/2 cup peanut oil, habanero Tabasco, almonds, garlic, salt, brown sugar, chipotle chile, soy, and black pepper. Blend until smooth. Yield 3 cups.

Serves 8
Heat level: **1 2 3 4 5 6 7 8** 9 10

**Aji panka is a chile from the Andes and can be ordered from specialty sources on the web; it really has no substitute.*

Sun-Dried Tomato Salsa / ITALY

Sun-dried tomatoes became a huge fad way back in the 1970s when Dean & Deluca of New York first introduced them to the U.S. market. They were exotic, expensive, and magical, packed in beautiful small jars in olive oil so you could see the scarlet sun-dried fruit from Italy. American chefs had never experienced such an intense tomato flavor. Sun-dried tomatoes popped up in pastas, in salads, in breads, in soups—they were the darling ingredient of the year. Two generations later, sun-dried tomatoes are still a staple of the gourmet pantry. We have many different sun-dried tomatoes available, of varying qualities. The best ones are soft and velvety, not too salty, and packed in high-quality olive oil. Choose sun-dried tomatoes that are nonsulfured. This salsa has a number of other intense ingredients to balance and fill out the flavor dimensions. It's not an everyday salsa but for special meals.

1/3 cup white wine (Pinot Blanc)
2 cloves garlic, sliced thin
1/2 teaspoon saffron
1/4 teaspoon salt
1/2 cup bell chile (about 8)*
1 jar (10 ounces) sun-dried tomatoes in oil (Roland brand)
1/4 cup cippolini onion, cut in thin strips (1 medium)
1/2 teaspoon dried, crushed pepperoncini
1 teaspoon finely julienned or zested candied orange peel
1/4 teaspoon saffron, crushed
1 tablespoon orange juice
1 teaspoon white balsamic vinegar
1 tablespoon olive oil (Frantoni brand)

In a small saucepan, place the wine, garlic, 1/2 teaspoon saffron, and salt and cook for 3 minutes or until liquid is reduced to 2 tablespoons; reserve. Fire roast the bell chile. Place in a plastic bag to steam. When cool, peel, deseed, and cut in thin strips. Place in a bowl.

Drain the sun-dried tomatoes and reserve the oil. Cut tomatoes in thin strips. Place in bowl with chile. Fry the onion in the oil from the tomatoes until golden brown. Drain and add to the bowl. Add the reserved wine mixture, pepperoncini, candied orange peel, 1/4 teaspoon saffron, orange juice, balsamic vinegar, and olive oil. Yield 2 cups.

Serves 6
Heat level: **1 2 3 4** 5 6 7 8 9 10

**You can substitute Fresno.*

Verde Trio Salsa / MEXICO

Most salsa verdes are just tomatillos and one kind of green roasted chile, usually jalapeños. This recipe is far more complex and captivating—it falls somewhere between a Latin green chile salsa, a chimichurri, and a fresh herbaceous European salsa. The reason is that the combination of these three chiles, each with their own distinct characteristics, creates a more complex flavor puzzle to unlock. The combination of three herbs together, which are not traditionally used in the same recipe, adds to its mystery and compounded scent. A valuable salsa for tacos, enchiladas, eggs, chicken, and shrimp, this is also great for splashing on a dish when you want a burst of fresh flavor and color.

4 cloves garlic
1 pound tomatillos, husked, rinsed in hot water 5 times
1/4 onion
2 cups canola oil
3 serrano chiles
3 jalapeño chiles
3 poblano chiles
1 teaspoon salt
1/2 teaspoon sugar
12 basil leaves
2 tablespoons cilantro leaves
8 tarragon leaves

Heat a large pot of water and bring to a boil. Add the garlic and boil for 8 minutes. After 3 minutes, add the tomatillos. After 5 minutes, add the onion. After the 8 minutes are up, finish by draining the water and ice shocking all ingredients in a strainer. Core the tomatillos and chop the onion to equal 2 tablespoons.

Heat the canola oil to 350 degrees F and oil roast the chiles separately (first the serranos, then the jalapeños, then the poblanos). Place chiles in plastic bags to steam. Once they are cool, peel and deseed. Save the chile oil for another use.

In a food processor, combine the boiled garlic, tomatillos, and onion. Add the chiles. Add the salt, sugar, basil, cilantro, and tarragon. Pulse to a smooth paste. Yield 3 cups.

Serves 8
Heat level: **1 2 3 4 5 6** 7 8 9 10

Tip: *Sort out your tomatillos by size before you cook them; start with the largest first in the pot, then add medium, then smallest to prevent overcooking or undercooking. This will preserve the right color and texture.*

Romesco / SPAIN

The most famous salsa of Spain, Romesco fuses ripe, rich, red roasted sweet peppers with fresh peeled almonds, golden olive oil, and aromatic sweet garlic. It's all pounded together in a wooden mortar with a pestle to create a thick, luscious, velvety salsa for serving alongside grilled calsots—the baby leeks of early spring—or any of another dozen Spanish dishes that it usually accompanies. There are many salsas throughout the world that use nuts and/or seeds to create a more flavorful, more nutritious, and richer salsa. Pestos of northern Italy contain pine nuts, for example, and the pipians of Mexico contain roasted pumpkin seeds that are pounded with dried or fresh roasted chiles. The Balinese use the buttery candlenut of Indonesia in some of their recipes, and the Hawaiians use the macadamia nut in some of their salsas. Peanuts are used in the famous Thai peanut salsa that goes on their satays.

1 cup Spanish olive oil
10 ounces red bell peppers*
8 Fresno chiles
5 ounces Marcona blanched almonds
3 cloves garlic
1/4 cup Spanish olive oil
2 tablespoons plain breadcrumbs
2 1/2 teaspoons sherry vinegar
1 teaspoon Pimenton de la Vera, picante
1/2 teaspoon Pimenton de la Vera, dulce
1 tablespoon tomato paste
2 1/2 teaspoons salt

Heat 1 cup olive oil to 350 degrees F and fry the bell peppers and the Fresnos for 2 minutes, turning often. The oil may splatter; a frying screen is recommended. Place the bell pepper and chiles in a plastic bag to steam. When cool, peel and deseed.

Place the peppers and Fresnos in a food processor. Add the almonds, garlic, 1/4 cup olive oil, breadcrumbs, sherry vinegar, Pimenton picante, Pimenton dulce, tomato paste, and salt. Pulse until a smooth paste is obtained. In a mortar, place 1/2 cup salsa and mash further. This helps to crush any pieces that did not emulsify. Remove and repeat with remaining salsa, 1/2 cup at a time. This is an important and integral final step. The food processor helps to speed the process, but the salsa should be crushed in a mortar. Yield 2 cups.

Serves 6
Heat level: **1 2 3 4** 5 6 7 8 9 10

**Bottled red bell peppers or picillo peppers may be substituted.*

Harissa / MOROCCO

Harissa is one of my favorite salsas of all time: to taste it is to experience a volcano of exotic spices and perfumes. One whiff, one nibble, and you will be transported on a magic carpet to the fabled souks of Marrakech or the open, odorous spice markets of Fez, the sunny sea-sprayed Agadir, or the middle atlas mountains of Morocco. It is a sauce of mystery, with enigmatic flavors that are hypnotizing, like staring at the ceilings and tiles of the great mosques or disappearing into old Persian carpets. Although this recipe may not look accessible, you just have to start and continue on faith that it will all be worth it in the end. Trust me, it will. Making this recipe will give you the confidence to make that breakout from an ordinary cook to a magician in the kitchen.

3 Fresno chiles, sliced in rings, with seeds
1/2 cup rice wine vinegar
1/2 cup water
1/4 teaspoon salt
1 jar (10 ounces) sun-dried tomatoes in oil, drained (Roland brand)
1/2 clove garlic
1 1/2 teaspoons salt
1 teaspoon zested cured lemon peel
5 tablespoons Moroccan olive oil
1 tablespoon tomato paste, double concentrate (Whole Foods)
4 teaspoons Aleppo (Turkish hot pepper flakes or New Mexico red)
1 1/2 teaspoons Tabasco
1 teaspoon chipotle en adobo sauce
1 teaspoon ground caraway seeds
3/4 teaspoon ground fennel seeds
1 teaspoon ground coriander
1/2 teaspoon ground cayenne
3/4 teaspoon ground cumin
1/2 teaspoon ground cinnamon
3/4 teaspoon ground green anise seeds
1/4 teaspoon ground grains of paradise
1/4 teaspoon ground long pepper
1/4 teaspoon Pimenton de la Vera, picante
1/8 teaspoon black pepper

In a medium saucepan, place the sliced Fresnos with the rice wine vinegar, water, and 1/4 teaspoon salt. Cook until soft, over medium heat, about 10 minutes. Place in a food processor with the sun-dried tomatoes. Puree until smooth. Add the garlic, 1 1/2 teaspoons salt, lemon peel, olive oil, tomato paste, Aleppo chile flakes, Tabasco, chipotle sauce, caraway, fennel, coriander, cayenne, cumin, cinnamon, anise, grains of paradise, long pepper, Pimenton, and black pepper. Puree until smooth. Using a coarse wire mesh strainer, pass the Harissa through to obtain a fine puree. Yield 2 cups.

Serves 8
Heat level: **1 2 3 4 5 6 7 8** 9 10

Agrodolce / ITALY

Bitter and sweet tastes combine in this salsa in a complex, satisfying composition. Each taste defines the other by being the perfect contrast. The trick is to get the right balance between the savory, spicy elements and the sweet, sugary ones. This recipe is Italian-inspired, and its history goes back to Roman days when they used garum as an accent in their cooking. Garum was a condiment made from fermented anchovy or fish sauce and used much like we use soy sauce today. It was combined with vinegar and sweet fruits in some of their more sumptuous dishes. The current regional cuisine of Sicily still has many dishes with those same flavors: a good example is the famous pasta Sardine in Soar—fresh or canned sardines cooked with vinegar and sweet golden raisins, combined with pine nuts, and sauced on top of al dente pasta with garlicky golden breadcrumbs as a finishing flourish and texture.

3 onions
1 tablespoon chestnut honey
1/4 cup white balsamic vinegar
1/2 teaspoon salt
1/4 cup golden raisins
2 tablespoons currants
1 cup Verjus or white wine
1/4 teaspoon saffron
2 cayenne chiles, dried, cut with scissors in thin rings
3/4 teaspoon finely minced rosemary
4 cloves smoked or roasted garlic, cut in quarters (see page 185)
1 teaspoon candied orange peel
2 ounces tuna, packed in oil with jalapeño
6 anchovies, packed in salt and olive oil
1 teaspoon white balsamic vinegar

Preheat oven to 450 degrees F. Line a heavy-bottomed casserole dish with parchment paper. Place the onions with skins on, root side up, in the dish and bake for 2 hours. The skins will caramelize and burn. Let cool. Peel away burnt skin and use the interior of the onion and any outer later that is not black. Dark sections are preferred. Slice lengthwise and place in a sauté pan. Add chestnut honey, 1/4 cup white balsamic vinegar, and salt. Cook until liquid has evaporated. Place in a mixing bowl.

In a saucepan, place the raisins, currants, Verjus or white wine, saffron, and chile rings. Cook over medium heat until liquid has evaporated. Add to the bowl with the onions. Add the rosemary, smoked garlic, and orange peel. Mix well. Flake the tuna in large pieces over the salsa and layer with the anchovies. Finish with a sprinkle of white balsamic vinegar. Yield 2 cups.

Serves 6
Heat level: **1 2** 3 4 5 6 7 8 9 10

Meyer Lemon, Jalapeño Kosho / JAPAN

This recipe is based on a famous Japanese ingredient called yuzu kosho. It's a paste made from crushed, roasted green chiles mixed with yuzu (lemony Japanese citrus), and sold in small jars. Yuzu kosho is used in yakitori recipes and in robata grilling. You can buy yuzu kosho at Japanese grocery stores, but it is hard to find away from cities with large Japanese populations like Los Angeles, San Francisco, and Seattle. Yuzu kosho is very expensive, so I created this homemade version of my own and it works very well, especially on chicken and seafood. Try to find Meyer lemons for this recipe, as they have a better perfume and give a more yuzu-like complexity to the salsa. Yuzu is becoming more widely available in the U.S. and very popular with exotic cocktails made by the creative mixologists, so look for it at your favorite cocktail hangout.

12 jalapeños, cut in half lengthwise
2 tablespoons Fleur de Sel, Gris, ground
1 ounce kombu (sea vegetable), thin sheets
1 1/4 cured Meyer lemon
1/2 teaspoon Fleur de Sel, Gris
2 tablespoons Meyer lemon juice

Preheat oven to 400 degrees F. Sprinkle each jalapeño half with about 1/8 teaspoon ground Fleur de Sel, Gris. Place jalapeños in a medium nonstick pan and bake for about 40 minutes. The salt has a curing effect and pulls the water from the jalapeños. When cool, remove the seeds. Place on a cutting board and mince fine with any salt that is left in the pan. Place the kombu in 1 tablespoon water and let hydrate, about 15 minutes. If very dry, use an additional tablespoon water. Chop very fine. Remove the pith and any white part from the cured lemons and mince fine. Bring the three ingredients together and continue to chop. Add the coarse 1/2 teaspoon Fleur de Sel and use the tip of the knife to make a paste. Add the lemon juice. Yield 1 cup.

Serves 8
Heat level: **1 2 3 4 5 6** 7 8 9 10

Rouille / FRANCE

Rouille is traditionally served with bouillabaisse, the famous multilayered fish and shellfish stew from the South of France, particularly Marseilles. This is a very luxurious lobster rouille from the lobster roe and claw meat. Lobster roe is fairly easy to obtain and works well. When the bouillabaisse is served, a bowl of rouille is served alongside with toasted bread. You spoon the rouille into your soup and stir it in to provide an extra level of spice and intensity of seafood aromas and richness. Add the rouille at the end when you finish your dish.

1 1/2 pounds female lobster
4 cups water
1/2 onion, chopped
1 carrot, chopped
1/4 cup chopped fennel fronds and stalks
1/2 teaspoon saffron
1 clove garlic
1/2 teaspoon salt
1/2 Yukon potato, peeled, sliced thick
2 cloves garlic
1/4 teaspoon sea salt
1 egg yolk, room temperature
1 roe from lobster, cooked
2 tablespoons lobster stock
1/2 teaspoon New Mexico red chile, dried, crushed or 1/8 teaspoon cayenne
1/2 cup olive oil
1 cup rough chopped lobster meat (approximately)

Ask your fishmonger for a female lobster weighing 1 1/2 pounds. Place the 4 cups water in a large pot with a lid. Add the onion, carrot, fennel, saffron, 1 clove garlic, and 1/2 teaspoon salt. Heat to a simmer for about 5 minutes, then increase the heat to medium and add the lobster. Cook for 12 minutes. Remove the lobster to an ice bath. When cool, remove the roe from the tail. Remove the meat, claw meat, and knuckle meat; reserve. Add the shells and body back into the pot and cook for 20 minutes.

In a blender, blend the lobster stock and strain through a fine sieve. Return to pot. Add the potato slices. When cooked and cooled, mash 2 tablespoons potato; reserve. In a large mortar, place the 2 cloves garlic and sea salt and mash to a fine paste. Add the egg yolk and roe from the lobster and grind, again to a fine paste. Add the reserved potato, lobster stock, and New Mexico red chile powder. Continue to make a paste. Add 1 teaspoon of olive oil and start the emulsion. Continue to add the oil very slowly, until it is completely incorporated. Fold paste into the chopped lobster meat. Yield 1 1/2 cups.

Serves 8
Heat level: **1 2 3 4** 5 6 7 8 9 10

3 | Classic Dried Chile Salsas

Puya (Pulla) / MEXICO

The puya chile is one of my favorites from which to make dried chile salsa, since it is not as hot as the arbol and has more flavor than just a plain dried guajillo or dried New Mexico chile. It is dark red mahogany in color and about 3 1/2 inches long by 1 inch across. The flavor profile of the puya is dark and lightly sweet, somewhat cherry and smoky with a long finish. It pairs well with anchor or cascabel chiles and is great with hearty meat dishes. For those who like a rounder, less fiery chile salsa they should try this one.

2 ounces puya chiles (about 40)
1 tablespoon puya chile seeds
3 cups water
4 cloves garlic
1/2 white onion
9 ounces cherry tomatoes
1 teaspoon Chipotle Tabasco
1 teaspoon kosher salt

Heat a comal or cast iron pan to medium-low heat. Roast the chiles to make them more pliable. Remove the seeds and place in a small bowl. Discard the stems and remove any veins. Return 1 tablespoon of the seeds to the pan and roast for 1 to 2 minutes, making sure not to burn them. Reserve.

Place the chiles in a saucepan and add the water. Bring to a boil and cover with a lid. Let simmer slowly for 20 minutes until liquid has reduced to 2 cups. Place the garlic and onion in the comal or cast iron pan and slowly roast for 15 minutes. Remove. Chop onion and measure 1/2 cup; reserve.

Heat the comal or cast iron pan to high heat and blacken the tomatoes for 6 to 7 minutes. In a blender, add the chiles in water, garlic, onion, blackened tomatoes, Chipotle Tabasco, salt, and roasted seeds. Blend 4 minutes on low speed then 5 minutes on high speed. Yield 2 cups.

Serves 8
Heat level: **1 2 3 4 5 6** 7 8 9 10

Guajillo / MEXICO

The guajillo is the most widely used dried chile in Mexico; it is fleshy enough to give a good yield, easy to work with, and has some heat and a good amount of flavor. It is used extensively in enchilada and red chile sauces, in posoles, and in moles. It is a larger relative of the puya chile and widely available. About 6 inches long by 2 inches wide, the guajillo has a light cherry tomato/grassy flavor profile with medium heat. Pairing guajillo chiles with arbol chiles gives a salsa some bite and makes it more complex.

4 ounces guajillo chiles
4 arbol chiles
1 tablespoon seeds from guajillo and arbol chiles
3 cups water
4 cloves garlic
1/2 white onion
1/2 cup cherry tomatoes
2 1/4 teaspoons salt
1 tablespoon red wine vinegar
1 teaspoon agave nectar (Madhava brand)

Preheat a cast iron pan or comal to medium-low. Stem and seed the guajillo and arbol chiles. Combine the seeds and toast 1 tablespoon of the seeds for 2 minutes, making sure not to burn. Reserve.

Toast the guajillo and arbol chiles for 2 minutes. Place in a saucepan with the water. Bring to a boil and cook for 10 minutes or until liquid is reduced to 1 1/2 cups.

Roast the garlic and onion in the cast iron pan or comal on medium-low for 15 minutes. Increase the heat to medium-high and roast the tomatoes for 6 minutes. Chop the onion and measure 1/2 cup. Place the tomatoes, onion, garlic, and cooked chiles in a blender and mix for 4 minutes on low speed. Add the toasted seeds, salt, red wine vinegar, and agave nectar and blend on high speed for 4 minutes until a smooth puree is achieved. Yield 2 cups.

Serves 6
Heat level: **1 2 3 4 5** 6 7 8 9 10

Tip: *Because chiles are fruits and not vegetables, you develop more complex flavors when you blend more than one variety of chile into a salsa. Each chile has a distinctive profile and it's the combination of chiles that makes a great salsa, just like it's a combination of varieties of grapes that makes a more interesting wine.*

Katarina / MEXICO

The Katarina chile is a medium-hot chile from central Mexico with lots of cherry fruity tones; it makes an excellent general table salsa. It is thin-skinned and elongated, about 2 1/2 inches long by 3/4 of an inch wide. The Katarina is a rare chile, but because it has such clear fruity notes it is worth seeking out.

1 ounce Katarina chiles, dried (about 30)
1 tablespoon Katarina seeds
1 1/2 cups water
10 cloves garlic
2 white onions
8 ounces tomatillos, rinsed 5 times (see page 120)
8 ounces cherry tomatoes
1 teaspoon salt
1/4 teaspoon smoked salt
1/4 teaspoon sugar
1 teaspoon salsa de bruja vinegar (see page 180)
1 teaspoon olive oil

BAY LEAF SALT

1 bay leaf ground in a mortar with 1/8 teaspoon salt

Preheat a nonstick pan and a cast iron pan to medium-low. Stem and deseed the Katarina chiles. Toast the seeds in the nonstick pan for 1 minute. Remove from the pan. Let cool and grind. Reserve. Toast the Katarina chiles for 2 minutes, turning often. Place in small saucepan and add the water. Simmer, covered, for 15 minutes. Add chiles and liquid to a food processor and blend to a smooth paste.

While the Katarinas are cooking, roast the garlic for 15 minutes in the cast iron pan. Roast the onions after the garlic for 12 minutes. Roast the tomatillos and cherry tomatoes in the nonstick pan while the onions are roasting in the cast iron pan.

In the food processor that has the Katarina chile puree, add the garlic, onion, tomatillos, tomatoes, salt, smoked salt, sugar, salsa de bruja, olive oil, and ground toasted seeds. Pulse for 2 minutes to a chunky salsa consistency. Place the salsa in a serving bowl and top with Bay Leaf Salt. Yield 3 cups.

Serves 8
Heat level: **1 2 3 4 5 6 7** 8 9 10

Taquero Taco Salsa / MEXICO

This salsa is named after those proud taco masters of the street stands of Mexico, the Taquero, who can make a taco with one hand—assembling two fresh corn tortillas with their special meat and then throwing the fresh chopped white onions and cilantro over and across the top. They can make a taco in 8 seconds—now that's fast food! The Taquero can slice the meat off a revolving spit to make perfect tacos al pastor and catch a piece of grilled pineapple onto the taco without even looking. They must have an expertise in perfect cooking and dramatic showmanship, as well as having amiable personalities. It's just not the same when you get the assembly line version in the states. Taquero Taco Salsa is another good basic dried chile salsa that is more in the style of northern Mexico or Texas.

2 cloves garlic
1/2 white onion
14 ounces Roma tomatoes (about 6)*
6 whole chipotle chile peppers, en adobo (La Costeña brand)
1 tablespoon adobo sauce
6 tablespoons Chipotle Tabasco
1 teaspoon ketchup
1 tablespoon white vinegar
1/2 teaspoon salt
1/2 teaspoon brown sugar

In a cast iron pan or comal heated to medium-low, roast the garlic and onion for 15 minutes. Chop the onion and measure 1/4 cup. Over an open flame covered with a grill grate, fire roast the tomatoes. Place the garlic, onion, and tomatoes in a blender. Add the chipotle peppers and blend for 4 minutes on low. Add the adobo sauce, Chipotle Tabasco, ketchup, vinegar, salt, and brown sugar and blend on high speed for 4 minutes. Yield 2 cups.

Serves 8
Heat level: **1 2 3 4 5 6 7 8** 9 10

Note: *Canned tomatoes are perfectly suited for this recipe. Canned chipotles or those from the Basics chapter are completely interchangeable. All brands of dried chipotles in adobo are not equal: I have found the La Costeña brand to have the best flavor and not to be bitter. They have a more authentic smoky flavor.*

**Canned fire roasted tomatoes (Hunt's brand) may be substituted.*

Chipotle en Adobo / MEXICO

We all know and like the regular canned chipotle in adobo, which is dried smoked jalapeños that are pickled in vinegar and tomato sauce and then canned. But this homemade chipotle salsa version is light-years ahead. It has many more notes and flavors and is so much more complex—after having this salsa there is no going back! Think of it as the difference between white bread in a plastic bag from the grocery shelf and artisanal bread made from real grains taken fresh from a wood-burning oven. This is a great salsa to put on the table for tacos, as a dipping sauce for French fries, or as part of a raw bar. It goes well on sandwiches and you can puree it to create a basting sauce for BBQ, meats, or fish (try chipotle-glazed roasted fresh Alaskan salmon). Chipotle en Adobo gets better after storing it for a few days.

5 cloves garlic
2 ounces whole morita chiles, dried, stemmed, with seeds
8 cups water
1 1/4 cups white vinegar
2/3 cup thin sliced white onion
2 teaspoons smoked salt
3 whole allspice berries
1 thyme sprig or 1/4 teaspoon dried canella stick
3 tablespoons apple juice concentrate (Tree Top brand)
1/4 teaspoon liquid smoke (pecan)
1/4 cup ketchup (Heinz brand)
1/4 cup tomato paste
1 tablespoon sherry vinegar

In a cast iron pan or comal heated to medium-low heat, roast the garlic for 15 minutes and place in a medium saucepan. Toast the morita chiles for 2 minutes and add to the pan. Add the water, vinegar, onion, salt, allspice berries, thyme or canella, apple juice, and liquid smoke. Cook, covered, for 30 minutes on a low simmer. Add the ketchup and tomato paste and cook uncovered for 20 more minutes, until liquid has reduced to about 1 cup. Let cool and add the sherry vinegar. Yield 2 1/2 cups.

Serves 10
Heat level: **1 2 3 4 5 6 7 8** 9 10

Morita / MEXICO

The word chipotle *means a chile that is smoked; it is not a particular variety of chile as most people believe. There are eight different chiles in Mexico that are usually called chipotles and they are all a little different. The morita is one form of chipotle chile from Mexico. Most chipotles are dried smoked jalapeños, and their smoky flavor comes as the secondary result of drying the jalapeños over fires (the flesh of the jalapeño is too thick to dry naturally by hanging in the sun like most chiles). Drying chiles over fires also activates the capsaicin, so chiles treated in this way become hotter along with becoming smoky. Smoke is made up of a vast array of different essences, so it gives complexity to foods. This salsa has a captivating presence and depth; every time I make it someone asks for the recipe, saying it's the best BBQ sauce they have ever had.*

2 ounces morita chiles, stemmed, with seeds
8 cups water
1 clove garlic
1 small white onion
1/4 cup roasted cherry tomatoes (about 8)
1 tablespoon tomato paste
4 teaspoons ketchup (Heinz brand)
1 tablespoon Chipotle Tabasco
1/2 teaspoon kosher salt
3/4 teaspoon smoked salt
1 1/2 teaspoons brown sugar
1 teaspoon smoked chile oil (see page 93)
1 1/2 teaspoons sherry vinegar

In a cast iron pan or comal heated to medium-low, toast the morita chiles for 2 minutes. Place in a saucepan and add water. Bring to a boil and let cook, uncovered, for 30 minutes or until liquid is reduced to 2 cups. Place in a blender.

Roast the garlic and onion in the cast iron pan or comal for 15 minutes. Chop the onion and measure 1/2 cup. Add onion and garlic to the blender. Increase the heat to medium-high and dry roast the tomatoes. Add to the blender. Add the tomato paste, ketchup, Chipotle Tabasco, salt, smoked salt, brown sugar, chile oil, and sherry vinegar. Puree on high speed until no seeds are visible, about 6 minutes. Yield 3 1/2 cups.

Serves 8
Heat level: **1 2 3 4 5 6 7 8** 9 10

Arbol / MEXICO

The word arbol *means "like a tree" in Spanish and the chile bush that the arbol chile grows on has thick stalks almost like a tree. This salsa is the workhorse of dried chile salsas; it's used in almost every taco stand throughout Mexico and is the table salsa in many restaurants and* loncherias. *Arbol salsa is the basic model for all the common red chile salsas that you see in bottles everywhere, with or without fancy labels or tops, like Cahuilla. The addition of roasted pumpkin seeds along with the arbol seeds in this recipe gives the salsa a richer taste. It also provides some of the natural oil from the seeds, which makes the salsa thicker so it does not run.*

1 ounce arbol chiles, stemmed, with seeds (about 20)
2 1/2 cups water
1/2 teaspoon salt
4 teaspoons pumpkin seeds
3 cloves garlic
1/2 cup roasted cherry tomatoes (about 15)
2 teaspoons Tabasco
2 teaspoons white vinegar
1/2 teaspoon salt

In a cast iron pan or comal heated to medium-low, toast the arbol chiles for 2 minutes. Place the chiles in a saucepan. Add the water and 1/2 teaspoon salt. Bring to a boil and let cook for 15 minutes, covered, until liquid is reduced to 1 cup. Place in a blender. Roast the pumpkin seeds in the pan or comal until the seeds pop, about 3 minutes. Remove and reserve. Roast the garlic and tomatoes for 15 minutes and add to the blender. Add the reserved pumpkin seeds, Tabasco, vinegar, and 1/2 teaspoon salt. Blend until smooth. Yield 2 cups.

Serves 8
Heat level: **1 2 3 4 5 6** 7 8 9 10

Tip: *Try to find real arbol chiles and not the Japanese, Korean, or Chinese small red dried chiles that are more like chile cayenne. They are very hot, but with no subtle flavors. When you buy any dried chiles, make sure the color of the chile is bright cherry red and that they are not too dry; if they are too dry they will be too old and lose some of their fruitier tones.*

Tip: *When you toast the dried chiles, be careful not to burn them or the salsa will end up tasting scorched. When you toast the pumpkin seeds, make sure that there is only one level of seed in the pan, as they need to pop evenly. If the pan has too many seeds or the heat is too high they will burn or there will be too many seeds left unpopped.*

Tex-Mex / TEXAS/MEXICO

The predominant flavors that Texans like in their Mexican food are a rounded sweet smoky note and an aromatic woodiness that usually comes from cumin and oregano. This all-around salsa has that kind of profile and is another example of how many different regional versions of chile salsa there are in just one area. Most of these flavors were derived from the vaqueros, or the first cowboys of northern Mexico, who eventually settled in Texas and created the great cowboy culture of the West. If you cannot find morita chiles, you can use canned or dried chipotle (whole or powdered). I use only some of the seeds in each sauce, as too many seeds can create a bitter taste. Be careful not to burn them.

1 1/2 teaspoons cumin
1/2 teaspoon oregano
2 ounces New Mexico red chiles (hot), stemmed and seeded
1 tablespoon seeds from New Mexico red chiles
1 arbol chile, dried, stemmed, seeded
2 morita chiles, with seeds
8 cups water
10 cloves garlic
1/2 white onion
9 ounces Roma tomatoes (about 5)
1 3/4 teaspoons salt
1 teaspoon agave syrup (Madhava brand)

In a cast iron pan or comal heated to medium-low, toast the cumin and oregano for 1 minute. Remove and reserve. Toast the seeds from the New Mexico chiles for 1 minute, making sure not to burn. Remove and measure 1 tablespoon; reserve. Place the New Mexico red chiles, arbol chile, and morita chiles in the pan and toast for 2 minutes, turning often. Place the chiles in a saucepan and add the water. Bring to a boil and cook for 30 minutes or until liquid reduces to 2 cups.

Roast the garlic and onion for 15 minutes on medium-low and remove from the pan. Chop onion and measure 1/2 cup; reserve. Turn the heat up to medium-high and roast the tomatoes for 8 minutes, turning often. Transfer to a blender. Add the garlic, onion, and cooked chiles with liquid. Puree for 4 minutes on low speed. Add the cumin, oregano, toasted seeds, salt, and agave syrup and blend for 4 minutes on high speed or until no seeds are visible. Yield 4 cups.

Serves 8
Heat level: **1 2 3 4 5 6 7 8** 9 10

Tip: *I use agave syrup in my recipes when I want a touch of ripeness; it is less obstructive to the subtle chile notes and less noticeable than white processed sugars.*

Aleppo / SYRIA

The aleppo chile is exclusive to the great historical Templar city in northern Syria. Aleppo has one of the best-preserved medieval castles in the Mediterranean, which sits on a huge hill overlooking the city below. It also has the best intact non-tourist medieval souk, or market, in the Middle East. The chiles were brought to Aleppo in the sixteenth century by later European traders and incorporated into the Syrian cuisine. Aleppo chiles have a pleasing balance of sweet fruit tones, light smoke, and mild heat. The use of chiles in the Middle East is to give a background accent, not to be the dominant flavor in the dish. Aleppo marries well with lamb and fruit such as sun-dried tomatoes or golden raisins, as in this recipe. If you have never used aleppo chiles, check them out—they make a nice change from regular paprika.

1 teaspoon sesame seeds*
1/2 teaspoon dried thyme
6 tablespoons aleppo chile flakes
1 tablespoon olive oil
2 cloves garlic, chopped
1/4 cup chopped onion
2 ounces jarred sun-dried tomatoes
2 tablespoons golden raisins
2 teaspoons salt
3 cups water
2 tablespoons red wine vinegar

In a wire mesh strainer over an open low flame, or in a nonstick pan heated to low, toast the sesame seeds for 1 minute. Remove from heat. Grind in a spice mill; reserve. Toast the thyme and aleppo in a nonstick pan for 2 minutes. Remove and reserve. Place the olive oil in a medium saucepan; add the garlic and onion and sauté for 4 minutes over low heat. Add the thyme, aleppo, sun-dried tomatoes, golden raisins, salt, and water and cook for 15 minutes on a low simmer. Blend in a blender and add the red wine vinegar and ground sesame seeds. Yield 2 cups.

Serves 6
Heat level: **1 2 3 4** 5 6 7 8 9 10

**Buy sesame seeds at good organic grocery stores where they are stored in the refrigerator or where they have a regular turn in inventory. Often the ones you buy in regular grocery stores are rancid from being on the shelf too long. Keep sesame seeds refrigerated after opening.*

Chile Negro / MEXICO

This is the darkest of all the dried chiles—almost jet black in color. Sometimes called "chile pasilla," it has a subtle dark licorice tone and hints of smoke, coffee, and chocolate. It can have a medium to medium-high heat and gives dishes an earthy depth that can contrast quite well with seafood. It also goes well in long-cooked dishes and is indispensable in mole and the most complex sauces of Mexican cuisine. In this recipe, I am using the dark beer Negro Modello to leverage the earthiness of the chile. My favorite way to use this chile is in dishes that have huitlacoche and wild mushrooms. The chile negro is about 6 to 7 inches long by about 1 1/2 to 2 inches wide. Sometimes in California they mistakenly call fresh poblanos "chile pasilla," so don't just go by the name.

2 ounces chile negro chiles
2 cups water
1 1/2 cups Negro Modelo beer, reserve 3 tablespoons
6 cloves garlic
1/2 white onion
5 ounces cherry tomatoes
1 teaspoon kosher salt
1 teaspoon chile negro seeds
1/2 teaspoon Chipotle Tabasco

In a cast iron pan or comal, toast the chiles, then deseed and devein. Toast the seeds on medium-low heat and reserve. Put the chiles in the water and beer and bring to a boil; cook for 20 minutes or until liquid is reduced to 2 cups. Heat the cast iron pan or comal to medium-low and roast the garlic and onion for 15 minutes. Chop onion and measure 1/2 cup. Turn heat to medium-high and blacken the cherry tomatoes.

Put the chiles and liquid in a blender. Add the garlic, onion, cherry tomatoes, salt, 1 teaspoon toasted seeds, and Chipotle Tabasco. Blend on low speed for 4 minutes then on high speed for 5 minutes. When cool, add the reserved 3 tablespoons of beer. Yield 3 cups.

Serves 8
Heat level: **1 2 3 4 5 6 7** 8 9 10

4 | Tropical Salsas

Hainan / SINGAPORE

Everywhere at lunchtime in Singapore, the bustling city slows down. And everywhere from simple street stalls to ornate dining rooms in 5-star hotels, you will see thousands of diners ordering and enjoying this timeless satisfying dish. These salsas are multipurpose and can be used as dipping sauces for BBQ Asian ribs, dumplings, fried fish, raw oysters, and endless possibilities.

GINGER SALSA

2 1/2 ounces ginger
2 tablespoons fine minced lemongrass
2 teaspoons kosher salt
2 teaspoons sugar
2/3 cup soy oil or canola oil
2 tablespoons rice wine vinegar (Marukan brand)
2 tablespoons lime juice
1/4 cup rough chopped cilantro

On a fine Microplane, grate the ginger and place in a mortar. Add the lemongrass. Add the salt and sugar. Using the pestle, make a fine paste. Heat the oil to 375 degrees F and pour over the ginger and lemongrass mixture. Let cool completely. Add the rice wine vinegar, lime juice, and cilantro. Yield 1 cup.

CHILE SALSA

1 tablespoon grated ginger
1 tablespoon grated garlic
3 Thai red chiles
1/2 teaspoon kosher salt
1 teaspoon sugar
6 tablespoons soy oil
4 tablespoons chile oil
1/2 cup sambal oelek
1/2 cup tomato paste (Hunt's brand)
2 teaspoons Sriracha chile sauce
4 teaspoons lime juice
3 tablespoons rice wine vinegar (Marukan brand)
1/4 cup water

On a fine Microplane grate the ginger, garlic, and Thai chiles. Place in a mortar. Add the salt and sugar. Using a pestle, make a fine paste. Heat the soy and chile oils to 375 degrees F and pour over ginger, garlic, and chile mixture. Let cool completely. Add the sambal oelek, tomato paste, Sriracha sauce, lime juice, rice wine vinegar, and water. Yield 1 cup.

SWEET SOY

1 clove garlic
6 tablespoons light soy (low sodium)
2 tablespoons sweet soy sauce
5 tablespoons seasoned rice wine vinegar (Marukan brand)
2 tablespoons sesame chile oil
1 1/2 teaspoons sugar
1 tablespoon lime juice

On a truffle slicer, slice the garlic paper thin. Add the light soy, sweet soy sauce, rice wine vinegar, sesame chile oil, sugar, and lime juice. Yield 1 cup.

Serves 8
Heat level: **1 2 3 4**

Roasted Pineapple Habanero Salsa / MEXICO

This is definitely one of the all-time Hall of Fame salsas that I have created; it has that blend of sweet tropical hot and searing habanero that is addictive. Whenever we add this to a salsa bar, we have to make double as it's the first one to go. It's perfect for all grilled seafood, tacos al pastor, sopes, and tostadas, as well as for garnishing salads.

1 pineapple (about 18 ounces)
1 habanero chile
1 cup diced mango
2 tablespoons lime juice

Heat a heavy bottomed nonstick pan to medium-low. Peel the pineapple, cleaning it with a thin-bladed knife with long strokes. Follow the contour of the pineapple from top to bottom, curving in at the bottom and going deep enough to remove the black eyes. Cut out the core with a circular cutter. Cut the pineapple into 1/2-inch rings. Place in the preheated pan and let roast for 6 to 8 minutes per side. When the pineapple is cool, dice in 1/4-inch pieces and place in a bowl. Dry roast the habanero chile for 12 minutes. When cool, wearing gloves, mince the habanero with seeds and place in the bowl. Peel and cut the mango in 1/4-inch cubes and add to the bowl. Add the lime juice and mix well. Yield 3 cups.

Serves 6
Heat level: **1 2 3 4 5 6 7**

Koh Samui, Lemongrass Mango / THAILAND

Koh Samui is one of those dreamlike tropical islands, off the southern coast of Thailand. It is blessed with swaying palms, balmy winds, turquoise waters, and pristine white sandy beaches, with hardly any signs of modern industrial life. You arrive and leave by water taxis from the airport and are willingly marooned for a week or so, if you are lucky. The dishes of this island are as striking in their multihued flavors as the markings of tropical fishes.

4 teaspoons fine minced lemongrass
4 Thai red chiles
1 pound mangos (about 3 medium)
10 Thai basil leaves
1 tablespoon grated palm sugar
1 lime, juiced

Place the lemongrass in a bowl. Slice the Thai chiles in rings and add. Peel the mangos and remove the fruit from the pit; dice in 3/8-inch pieces. Add to salsa. To get all the mango off the pit, use a grater on the biggest grate and press the pit against the grater. This will give a puree. Add to salsa. Place the Thai basil leaves one on top of each other and roll in a tube. Slice across, fine, and add to the salsa. Add the grated palm sugar and lime juice. Yield 2 cups.

Serves 6
Heat level: **1 2 3 4 5** 6 7 8 9 10

Tip: *When you buy lemongrass, make sure that it is fresh and moist and that the root has not been grown out too many times. Sometimes they cut the stalks above ground and leave the rootstalk to send up more shoots; eventually the rootstalk is too tough to use. So break a stalk at the base and look at the bottom of the lemongrass stalk—there should be no thick brown rings, just pale, very light yellow flesh that is very moist and has robust perfume. Also, it helps to use a clean spice mill to chop lemongrass very, very fine. Lemongrass will oxidize within a couple of hours, so only prepare what you can use quickly or you will lose the appearance and also the perfume.*

Tip: *Palm sugar is easy to buy in any Asian grocery store and it's a totally natural product that stores well. If you cannot find it, you can substitute half light brown sugar with half processed white sugar.*

Thai Basil Pineapple / THAILAND

Nowhere in the world is there such an abundance of exotic ripe tropical fruit as there is in Thailand. You can't walk down a sidewalk without passing either a vendor's cart with fresh fruit on ice—ruby wedges of watermelon, carved golden pineapple, pale lemon jungle apples, or saffron mangos—or baskets heaped with fresh fruit spilling onto the sidewalk from the stores. The mangosteens, fresh lychees, and dragon fruits are colored like wild parrots, and the scarlet hairy rambutans have the lusciousness of a white peach mixed with lychee with a little pineapple thrown in. The supermarkets are also loaded with fruit and pure fruit juice, the ripe aromas like a perfume tidal wave engulfing the senses. This salsa is a cross of two Thai passions: chiles and tropical fruit brought together with kaffir lime and lemongrass accents.

1 golden pineapple (about 18 ounces)
2 teaspoons fine minced lemongrass
2 Thai red chiles
2 Thai green chiles
1 kaffir lime leaf (or lime zest from 1 lime)
2 tablespoons Thai basil leaves (about 15)
1/2 teaspoon sugar
1 teaspoon fish sauce (3 Crabs brand)*
1 tablespoon lime juice

Peel and core the pineapple, then dice in 3/8-inch pieces and place in a bowl. Add the lemongrass to the bowl. Slice the red and green Thai chiles in rings and add. Remove the vein from the kaffir lime leaf and cut in fine julienne. Add to the salsa. To cut the Thai basil, place the leaves one on top of each other in the same direction, then roll in a tube and slice thinly across. Add to salsa. Add the sugar, fish sauce, and lime juice. Yield 2 cups.

Serves 6

Heat level: **1 2 3 4 5 6 7** 8 9 10

Tip: *Look to buy real kaffir lime leaves in large Asian markets, especially Thai markets, or in specialty markets like Kalustyan's that carry them in the freezer section. Buy as many as you think you can use during a six-month period and put them into ziplock freezer bags; they keep well and are hard to find regularly. Kaffir lime leaves create a unique scent that is not quite duplicable by any other substitute.*

**Fish sauce is the salt component. Use to taste.*

Papaya Habanero / CARIBBEAN

The word habanero *means "from Havana," where presumably this chile came from on its culinary journey to southern Mexico. It is a member of the tropical capsicum Chinese family of chiles that originated in the Caribbean. The habanero is commonly used across the Yucatán of Mexico and it was here that I first learned to embrace its fiery kiss. I was having a taco of cochinita pobil in the Merida market and lavishly added a large spoonful of lightly pickled yellow strips to my tortilla. I usually associate the color yellow with bananas, pineapple, and mangos—harmless, enjoyable foods. Not this time! The inferno on my tongue set off, and my reaction to get rid of the remaining food was too slow to stop the ensuing forest fire. My palate had been firebombed and it was still smoldering twenty minutes later! The arsonist was the habanero chile, and since then I have held that chile in respect and know how to contain its explosive aspect while leveraging its tropical character.*

1 habanero
1 mango
2 1/2 cups diced papaya
2 teaspoons grated ginger
2 teaspoons sugar
1/2 teaspoon fresh ground mace
1 lime, zested
3 tablespoons lime juice
1 tablespoon papaya seed juice*

In a cast iron pan or comal heated to medium-low, roast the habanero for 8 minutes. When cool, deseed and mince; reserve. Peel and cut the fruit from the pit of the mango, then puree in a food processor and add the habanero. Remove from the processor and place in a bowl. Peel the papaya and cut in 3/8-inch pieces; add. Add the ginger. Add the sugar, mace, lime zest, lime juice, and papaya seed juice. Do not overmix this salsa as the papaya will break down easily. Yield 3 cups.

Serves 8
Heat level: **1 2 3 4** 5 6 7 8 9 10

Tip: *Look for the real spice mace, as it's more subtle than nutmeg and has lots of uses. Mace is actually the outer web that grows on the kernel of the whole nutmeg inside the fruit. It is a lighter essence than nutmeg, not so obvious and overbearing.*

**The seeds of the papaya have a taste similar to mustard. They can be juiced by placing the seeds in a fine mesh strainer and pressing with a spatula or ladle. They are also a digestive aid.*

Sweet Chile and Pineapple Salsa / THAILAND

Sweet and hot: classic partners. This is a very simple and quick salsa to make and is full of exploding flavors and colors. The pineapple has a bright tart-sweet juiciness and the sauce is a great accessory to dress up other dishes to add to their appeal. The coconut sugar has a softer sweetness that marries better with the rest of the fruit; it makes the pineapple seem riper rather than just sweeter, as is the case when using all white sugar. Sweet Chile and Pineapple Salsa is a great salsa to put out for the BBQ table with grilled chicken or pork, or even lobster.

3 stalks lemongrass, bruised
1 tablespoon rough chopped ginger
1 kaffir lime leaf, bruised*
6 tablespoons rough chopped Fresno chiles
1 clove garlic (optional if using pineapple)**
2 tablespoons sambal oelek
1 1/2 cups water
3/4 cup coconut sugar
1/2 cup sugar
1/4 cup honey
1 golden pineapple

Place lemongrass, ginger, and kaffir lime leaf in a cheesecloth and tie with a string. Put the Fresno chiles and garlic, if using, in a food processor and blend. Transfer to a medium saucepan and add sambal oelek, water, coconut sugar, sugar, honey, and cheesecloth containing the aromatics. Simmer for 10 minutes. Cut the pineapple into 10 equal sections and slice across 1/8 inch to make small fans (about 3 cups chopped). Pour hot sauce over pineapple. Yield 3 cups.

Serves 8
Heat level: **1 2 3 4 5 6** 7 8 9 10

**If you cannot find kaffir lime leaf, try using some very finely grated lime zest (Microplaned) from key limes as a substitute.*
***If you are making sweet chile dipping sauce without pineapple salsa, the garlic is an important ingredient. You may omit the garlic from the recipe if using pineapple.*

Jungle Curry Shrimp Salsa / THAILAND

This dish is an adaptation of one of the memorable appetizers that I eat all the time in northern Thailand at the idyllic, famous Four Seasons Chiang Mai resort. The enchanting markets of Chiang Mai contain the most remarkable array of dried fish products in the world. Your first contact with this mysterious, strongly fragrant section of the market is overwhelming. I was fortunate to have one of the world's experts on Thai Food, Naomi Duguid, as my guide. She has written extensively on Asian cuisine for years. Naomi explained that the use of different dried fish and fermented fish sauces creates the special unctuous umami characteristic in Thai dishes that make them so cravable and satiating. Here I use a combination of cooked jungle curry paste and raw curry paste to create an intricate web of flavors and aromas. I use this recipe to make Thai shrimp tacos. Or try it on a wonderful fresh lemongrass gazpacho as a garnish.

1 tablespoon canola oil
3 tablespoons Gaeng Pa, jungle curry, fried (see page 80)*
2 cups bay shrimp
1 tablespoon Gaeng Pa, jungle curry, uncooked*
3/4 cup cherry tomatoes
2 Thai chiles
1 kaffir lime leaf
1 tablespoon lime juice
1 teaspoon lemon oil

In a large nonstick sauté pan heated to high, add the oil and the prepared jungle curry and fry for 1 minute. Immediately add the shrimp and cook for 1 minute more. Remove to a large plate to cool. When the shrimp are cool, add the 1 tablespoon of uncooked jungle curry. Slice the cherry tomatoes in rings and add to the shrimp. Slice the Thai chiles in rings and cut the kaffir lime leaf in fine chiffonade; add. Juice the lime over the top and add the lemon oil. Yield 3 cups.

Serves 8
Heat level: **1 2 3 4 5 6** 7 8 9 10

**You can substitute the excellent jarred jungle curry pastes that you can find in the Asian section of most grocery stores.*

Gaeng Pa Jungle Curry / THAILAND

The word gaeng is the generic word for all "curry" dishes in Thailand. They are descended from Indian curry, but there is no confusing the two groups: the Thai Gaeng are like fireworks of fresh flavor and aromas; the Indian curries depend more upon dried spices. And each region of Thailand has its own specific flavor profile to its gaengs depending upon the topography and climate of the region. This jungle curry is from the northern part of Thailand, north of Chiang Mai. The cuisine of this region uses more ingredients from the woods such as roots, barks, wood, and berries than other culinary areas of Thailand. This salsa does have a lot of ingredients, but is very simple to make and has some of the most amazing, complex flavors of any salsa in the world. It is particularly good with pork, quail, pigeon, in wok dishes, and as an addition to Thai soups.

2 cloves garlic
3/4 teaspoon salt
2 tablespoons palm sugar
2 tablespoons dried shrimp, measured whole
3 tablespoons fine minced lemongrass
4 Thai red chiles
3 kaffir lime leaves
1 tablespoon grated galangal
1 teaspoon fresh grated turmeric
1 1/2 teaspoons grated ginger
1/2 teaspoon brown miso
1 teaspoon tamarind puree
1/2 teaspoon coriander seeds, ground
1 tablespoon fish sauce (3 Crabs brand)

Peel the garlic and place in a large mortar. Add the salt and smash until pureed. Add the palm sugar. In a spice mill, grind the dried shrimp then add to the mortar. Continue to make a puree with the pestle; after each addition continue mashing, working on the sides of the mortar. Add the lemongrass. Finely chop the Thai chiles and kaffir lime leaves and add to the salsa. Grate the galangal on a Microplane and add. Add the turmeric and ginger. Add the miso, tamarind puree, ground coriander, and fish sauce. Yield 1 cup.

Serves 8
Heat level: **1 2 3 4 5 6** 7 8 9 10

Tip: *I can always find galangal in Asian grocery stores; even the local Whole Foods in Santa Fe usually carries it. Galangal freezes quite well, and it's great to have around for your Thai cooking excursions. Make sure to check for any mold before you buy it.*

Thai Peanut Salsa

This salsa is going to go right to the top of your favorites list. It has a lot of ingredients, but can be made in about 20 to 30 minutes and it keeps well. Peanut salsas are found on every main street vendors' stand from Thailand to Singapore to Malaysia to Indonesia. If you go to a bar and order cocktails, often you will find small skewers of grilled pork or chicken served with this sauce to dip into. This version is so much better than the store-bought versions, which are dull and lifeless. Buy smooth, natural, organic peanut butter—it makes a big difference—and don't throw away the oil from the top. Fresh Market has a very good brand that I use at home. Also, it's very important not to add the liquid aromatics until the salsa is cool, otherwise they will make it taste more "muddy" and less distinct in the layered aromas.

2 tablespoons fine minced lemongrass
2 tablespoons fine minced shallot
2 teaspoons fine minced garlic
1 teaspoon fine grated galangal (grated on Microplane)
2 1/2 teaspoons ground dried Thai chile
1 tablespoon peanut oil
1 cup creamy organic peanut butter (Fresh Market brand)
1/2 cup water
1 cup coconut cream
1/4 cup sweet soy sauce
1/4 cup palm sugar
5 tablespoons tamarind paste
4 kaffir lime leaves, cut in fine threads
1 1/2 teaspoons fish sauce (3 Crabs brand)
1 1/2 teaspoons lime juice

Put the lemongrass, shallot, garlic, and galangal in a 12-inch sauté pan. Add the Thai chile and peanut oil and sauté on low heat for 5 minutes. Add the peanut butter, water, coconut cream, sweet soy sauce, palm sugar, and tamarind paste and let cook for 20 minutes. Let cool completely.

Add the kaffir lime leaves, fish sauce, and lime juice. Yield 2 1/2 cups.

Serves 8
Heat level: **1 2 3 4** 5 6 7 8 9 10

Banana Tamarind Sambal / THAILAND

Tamarind, which is extracted from a large pod of a shade tree, is used in many tropical areas of the world as a flavoring. It's used extensively in Indian chutneys, Mexican licuados, and Southeast Asian dishes. Tamarind has a natural sweet-sour taste that combines well with other flavors. As a matter of fact, it is probably one of the most recognized flavors in the world as it's used in cola soft drinks. Buy the tamarind pulp in the packages with the seeds as they are easy to prepare and the finished dish will taste better than if made with tamarind extract. Kalustyan's in New York does sell a natural tamarind extract that is very good, however.

2 tablespoons canola oil
2 kaffir lime leaves, cut in fine threads
1 cup diced shallot (small dice)
2 dried Thai red chiles, crushed
3 tablespoons diced Fresno chiles (3/8-inch dice)
3 tablespoons ground dried shrimp
1 tablespoon palm sugar
1 teaspoon sweet soy sauce
3 tablespoons tamarind puree
1 teaspoon lime juice
1 pound small red bananas*
2 tablespoons shredded coconut, toasted

Heat the oil on low heat in a sauté pan and fry the lime leaves for 10 seconds. Remove leaves and reserve. Fry the diced shallot in the oil until golden brown. At the end of cooking, add the dried chiles. This will yield about 1/2 cup fried shallot. Add the Fresno chiles to the shallots. In a spice mill, grind the dried shrimp and palm sugar and add to the shallot mixture. Add the sweet soy sauce, tamarind, and lime juice. Peel and cut bananas in 1/8-inch rounds and fold into shallot mixture. Fold in reserved fried kaffir lime leaves and coconut. Yield 3 cups.

Serves 8
Heat level: **1 2 3 4 5 6 7 8** 9 10

Tip: *To make tamarind paste from a block, cut 1/4 of the block and add 1 cup water and soften. Cook over low heat and strain. Then reduce to a thick paste.*

**Look for red tropical bananas or the tiny fingerling banana. Fingerling bananas are about double the size of your fingers; they have a much more pronounced banana flavor than regular bananas and are less starchy.*

Som Tom / NORTHEAST THAILAND

Every cuisine constantly evolves, as food is a living part of the culture. When I travel I am looking for new flavor compositions that I find pleasurable and fascinating, not just new dishes, and I am interested in the experiential part of the dish and not just the literal translations of ingredients and techniques. I want to always preserve the original balance and spirit of a dish and to do honor to and respect the food cultures that I am studying. This salsa was inspired from the celebrated Thai soup that everyone loves; the balance between sour and sweet, and fermented and spicy, makes it a fragrant, sensual masterpiece.

2 tablespoons minced shallot
2 teaspoons minced lemongrass
2 Thai green chiles, minced*
1 tablespoon dried shrimp, measured whole, ground in a spice mill
4 teaspoons palm sugar
1/4 teaspoon minced garlic
2 teaspoons tamarind puree
1 tablespoon lime juice
1 tablespoon fish sauce (3 Crabs brand)
1 tablespoon coconut water or water
1 kaffir lime leaf, cut in fine threads
2 cups green mango
1/2 cup cherry tomatoes
1 cup shredded green apple
10 Thai basil leaves, cut in julienne
1 tablespoon crushed dry roasted peanuts

Place the shallots in a mortar and make a paste with the pestle. After each of the following additions, work that ingredient into the paste: add the lemongrass, Thai chiles, ground dried shrimp, palm sugar, garlic, tamarind, lime juice, fish sauce, coconut water, and kaffir lime leaf. Place this mixture in a large mixing bowl.

Peel and cut the green mango into large shreds, about 1/4 inch x 5 inches, on a Benriner mandoline. Place in a mixing bowl with the marinade. Cut the cherry tomatoes in rings and add to the bowl. Peel and cut the apple into large shreds, about 1/4 inch x 5 inches, on a Benriner mandoline. Add. Cut the Thai basil in julienne by stacking the leaves and rolling in a tube, then slicing across fine. Add to the bowl. Sprinkle with roasted nuts before serving. Yield 3 cups.

Serves 8
Heat level: **1 2 3 4 5 6 7** 8 9 10

Tip: *When you buy dry roasted peanuts, look for very fresh ones in bulk and buy the unsalted ones as this dish has other salty elements. If you cannot find fresh roasted, buy some raw peanuts without skins and roast them yourself in a little peanut oil in the oven.*

5 | Smoky and Satisfying Salsas

Smoked Tofu Mustard Greens / CHINA

This salsa has its origin in the street foods of old Shanghai. I used to walk around the old historic city in the '80s and buy whatever food hit my fancy. I would eat it as I walked down through the old hutongs and street markets, which are now just a memory and have been replaced by contemporary sleek skyscrapers and a matrix of competing light shows on seventy-story buildings. One of my favorite local street foods at that time was the colossal white pillowy baos, or steamed buns, filled with dark smoked tofu and bright mustard greens. They were three to four times larger than the ones that I had eaten in San Francisco. Watching the white baos emerge from the enormous dark golden-stained bamboo baskets in which they were steamed was like watching an act of magic. This recipe makes an amazing vegetarian dish and also a fragrant stuffing for grilled quail.

TOFU

2 tablespoons hoisin
1 tablespoon organic soy
1 teaspoon premium soy
1 tablespoon sweet soy sauce
1 clove garlic, minced
1/2 teaspoon smoked salt
1/4 teaspoon white pepper
1 teaspoon Chinese red vinegar (Koon Chun brand)
1/2 teaspoon liquid smoke
1 tablespoon Chipotle Tabasco
1/2 teaspoon sugar
1 (10-ounce) firm tofu, sliced in 3 sections

Place the hoisin, organic soy, premium soy, sweet soy sauce, garlic, smoked salt, white pepper, vinegar, liquid smoke, Chipotle Tabasco, and sugar in a dish and marinate the cut tofu for 2 hours. Heat oven to 350 degrees F and bake tofu on parchment paper for 20 minutes using as much marinade as possible. Heat a grill to high and score the tofu with grill marks, turning, and repeat the grilling on both sides. When cool, cut into 1/2-inch cubes.

Continued on next page

Tip: *Make sure to look for firm, fresh tofu to make this dish, as regular tofu will disintegrate with so much handling.*

GREENS

2 cups mustard greens (about 2 bunches)
1 tablespoon soy oil or canola oil
1 clove garlic, minced
8 ounces shitake mushrooms
1/4 teaspoon white pepper
1/4 teaspoon smoked salt
1 tablespoon Chinese red vinegar (Koon Chun brand)
1 green onion, thin sliced, green part only

Devein the mustard greens and blanch in boiling salted water, then shock in salted ice water. Drain and cut into 1/2-inch pieces. Heat the oil in a sauté pan and add the garlic; let brown slightly. Stem the shitake and then cut the mushrooms in 1/2-inch pieces. Add the shitake, white pepper, and smoked salt to the pan and let cook for 4 minutes. Add the vinegar and let reduce until liquid has evaporated. Mix the tofu with the greens and mushroom mixture and add the sliced green onion. Yield 3 cups.

Serves 6
Heat level: **1 2 3 4 5** 6 7 8 9 10

Fig and Smoked Honey Salsa / SPAIN

Fig and Smoked Honey Salsa has complex smoky and sweet flavors. It uses a home smoker for the smoked honey—an inexpensive small model that you use on your stovetop, about the size of a small shoebox. These home smokers are readily available on the Web or in any of the large national camping/fishing stores. The honey you use in this recipe should be an interesting wild honey that is not too sweet or too bitter. Smoked honey is easy to make and is a great addition to your BBQ pantry. It's brilliant on grilled lobster and shrimp or an ideal finish to brush grilled baby back ribs or grilled chicken. We had this salsa with a marinated grilled leg of lamb off my home spit and it was amazing! It would also be magnificent with brined grilled quail.

2 cups figs (about 2 pints)
1/4 cup Pedro Ximenez sherry
3 tablespoons honey
1 cup diced sweet yellow onion (1/8-inch pieces)
2 tablespoons olive oil
3/4 teaspoon smoked salt
3 tablespoons fig balsamic vinegar
4 ounces Serrano ham, sliced thin

Preheat oven to 200 degrees F. Dice figs in 1/2-inch pieces and place in a 10-inch nonstick sauté pan. Pour Pedro Ximenez over the figs and bake for 1 hour, turning every 15 minutes. Let cool. Place honey in a low-rimmed container. Then place it in a stovetop smoker, using apple wood chips for smoke flavor. Start on high heat to ignite the smoke, then turn to low and let smoke for 10 minutes. Remove and reserve.

Sauté the onion in the olive oil. Season with smoked salt after the onion has turned golden brown. Add the fig balsamic vinegar and reduce until liquid has evaporated. Dice the sliced Serrano ham in 1/2-inch pieces. Combine the ham, onion, smoked honey, and figs. Yield 3 cups.

Serves 6
Heat level: 1 2 3 4 5 6 7 8 9 10

Breath of the Wok / CHINA

The intriguing flavor that captivates you when you dine on Chinese cuisine is not from one secret ingredient or one spice but from a composite flavor that is created from the proper "wok technique." This multifaceted perfume in Chinese cooking is referred to as "wok hei" or the "breath of the wok." It describes the flavor that is achieved when the wok vapors and flames combust together, then caramelize and enrobe the meat and other ingredients in a dense, intricate scent. The very best discussion of this process is in Grace Young's The Breath of the Wok, *one of the finest essential Chinese cookbooks ever to be written and highly recommended if you have any interest in cooking Asian food at home. The average commercial wok generates over 100,000 BTUs or more and is equal to the heat put out by ten or more home stove burners on their highest setting. So unless you have a commercial Chinese jet burner in your home, it's almost impossible to get the right "breath of the wok," on your food.*

2 cups soy oil or canola oil
1 cup Chinese long beans
1/2 cup soybeans
4 whole dried Arbol chiles
2 cloves garlic
2 tablespoons finely julienned ginger
1/4 cup diagonally sliced Chinese chives
2 tablespoons fermented black beans, rinsed in water
1/2 cup diagonally cut green onion (1/3-inch pieces)
1/4 teaspoon sugar
2 tablespoons light soy
1 teaspoon red wine vinegar
1/4 cup minced Chinese chives
1 tablespoon Chiu Chow chile oil (page 140)

Heat the oil in a wok to 375 degrees F and flash fry the long beans for 3 minutes. Remove to a paper towel to drain. Cut in 1/4-inch pieces. Blanch and drain the soybeans; reserve. Remove all except 2 tablespoons oil from the wok.

Get a prep plate and place the Arbol chiles on the plate in position number 1, garlic in position number 2, ginger in position number 3, chives in position number 4, black beans in position number 5, and green onions in position number 6. Set this plate aside.

Combine the sugar, soy, and vinegar and mix well; reserve. Heat the wok with the 2 tablespoons oil to high, until the oil starts to smoke. Working quickly, add the Arbol chiles and fry for 20 seconds, until browned; remove.

Add the garlic and after 10 seconds add the ginger. After 10 more seconds add the chives, black beans, and green onion. Cook for 20 seconds and add the long beans and soybeans. Cook for 20 more seconds, then add the soy mixture. Turn off heat and let cool. Add the minced chives, then dress with chile oil.

Having all the preparations ready is the most important part of making this salsa and achieving the wok barbeque smoke technique. Yield 3 cups.

Serves 6

Heat level: **1 2 3 4 5 6 7 8** 9 10

Tip: *To make this salsa, your best bet is to go to the Web and buy a portable outside Cajun burner made from a water heater gas ring. These burners can generate the requisite heat up to 200,000 BTUs. And if you use your wok outside you don't have to worry about the fumes. Also, many outside BBQ kitchens can accommodate this easily.*

Smoked Chile Oil / MEXICO

Perfect for your kitchen pantry, add this oil as a final seasoning to soups or salad dressings. Use it in stuffing or for meat marinades as well. Make sure to use a thermometer for the oil as you can burn the ingredients if the oil is too hot; and if the oil is too cold, it will not release the smoky perfumes.

18 cloves garlic
4 tablespoons morita chipotle chiles
1 tablespoon chipotle en adobo, chopped fine, without seeds
1 1/2 teaspoons smoked salt
3/4 cup canola oil

In a cast iron pan or comal, roast the garlic on medium-low heat for 15 minutes. In a spice mill, grind the morita chiles and place in a molcajete or 8-inch saucepan. Add the minced chipotle, garlic, and smoked salt. Grind to a paste. Heat the oil to 375 degrees F and pour over the top of chile-garlic paste. Let cool. Yield 1 cup.

Serves 12

Heat level: **1 2 3 4 5 6 7 8** 9 10

Avocado Bacon Jalapeño / TEXAS

I had to include a smoky salsa that highlights everyone's favorite smoky food of all time: bacon. Bacon is not just something that accompanies eggs in the morning anymore; it has moved from side dish to celebrity star. America has become infatuated with bacon—we live in an era of bacon mania! There are bacon swizzle sticks appearing in swanky martini bars, bacon ice cream for dessert in 3-star Michelin restaurants, and bacon being used as the main secret ingredient on Iron Chef. *It even appears in dainty cupcakes with caramel frosting. There are also "bacon of the month" clubs where each month for a year you receive seven different artisanal types of bacon (there are now more than 150 different bacons made in the United States) with a complete description of how they are made, what was used to do the smoking, and what heritage, natural, free-range breed was used.*

3 slices smoked center cut bacon
4 jalapeños
2 avocados
1 green onion, sliced in thin rings
3 tablespoons tangerine juice
1/2 teaspoon smoked salt
1 teaspoon Green Jalapeño Pepper Tabasco
1 teaspoon honey Dijon mustard

Preheat oven to 325 degrees F and cook the bacon on a wire rack with a drip pan for 12 to 14 minutes. The bacon is done when it is still slightly chewy and juicy; crispy bacon is not recommended. When cool, cut the bacon into 1/3-inch dice.

Over an open flame with a grill plate, fire roast the jalapeños. Place in a plastic bag to steam. When cool, peel, deseed, and dice in 1/4-inch pieces. Peel and remove the pit from the avocados; place the flesh in a mixing bowl. Add diced bacon, diced jalapeños, tangerine juice, smoked salt, Tabasco, and mustard and mix. Yield 2 cups.

Serves 6
Heat level: **1 2 3 4** 5 6 7 8 9 10

Tip: *Look for center cut bacon. It contains a lot less fat and more meat than average bacon. Try to get nitrate-free bacon if you can source it. If you can find jalapeño bacon, even better. This salsa is delectable with BLTs.*

Chipotle Rojo, Smoked Tomato, Fresno / MEXICALI

The smoky red of this salsa is taken from the two main ingredients: red Fresno chiles and red ripe Campari tomatoes. Campari tomatoes are small, vine-ripened tomatoes that are about 2 1/2 to 3 inches in diameter and are picked off the vine when they are fully ripe. The tomatoes have to be small enough to have the right proportion of charred skin to give the recipe the right amount of smoky flavor. They also have to be ripe enough to give the dish the natural sweetness that marries well with the ripe Fresno chiles. As with many chile salsas, the theme of sweet and hot is a great counterpoint in dishes. This recipe makes a great sandwich spread or is perfect for a dip. Try it on chilled fresh-cooked gulf shrimp or as a filling for quesadillas or even stirred into scrambled eggs.

8 cloves garlic
1 onion
4 Fresno chiles
1 pound Campari tomatoes (about 10)
1 1/2 teaspoons smoked salt
1/4 teaspoon sugar
1 teaspoon rice wine vinegar
1 chipotle en adobo, seeded
1 1/2 teaspoons chipotle en adobo sauce

In a cast iron pan or comal heated to medium-low, roast the garlic and onion for 15 minutes to ensure extra darkening. Place in a food processor. Fire roast the Fresnos and tomatoes. Remove the seeds from the Fresnos, but leave the skins on, and place both in the food processor. Add the smoked salt, sugar, vinegar, whole chipotle, and adobo sauce and process for 3 minutes, making a fairly smooth salsa. Yield 2 1/2 cups.

Serves 8
Heat level: **1 2 3 4 5 6 7** 8 9 10

Note: *You can substitute fresh long red Hot Dutch peppers in this recipe if you cannot find Fresno chiles.*

Tomatillo Morita / NORTHERN MEXICO

This is one of the standard classics of the Mexican kitchen, perfect on almost everything from tostadas to tacos. The word chipotle *is derived from two words in the pre-Hispanic language Nuatl of Mexico. The first part* chi, *meaning "chile," and the second part* potle, *meaning "smoky." So the word* chipotle *means any chile that is smoked. There are eight different varieties of smoked chiles in Mexico, including dried chiles and processed smoked chiles such as the common chipotles en adobo that you find on the grocery aisles. This recipe uses the variety morita. The morita chile has an intense, sweet smoky flavor that is closer to a mild BBQ flavor. The advantage to using a dried variety of chile rather than the canned ones is that you can control the flavor more. Also the canned ones have vinegar and sugar added, which make them hotter than you may want. Dried chiles also give you a darker, more earthy sauce.*

1 1/4 ounces morita chipotle chiles*
2 cups water
4 cloves garlic
1 small white onion
1 pound tomatillos, washed 5 times and cored
1/2 teaspoon salt
3/4 teaspoon smoked salt
1/2 teaspoon brown sugar
2 teaspoons Chipotle Tabasco

In a cast iron pan or comal heated to medium-low, toast the morita chiles for 2 minutes. Remove the seeds and place in a saucepan with 2 cups of water; simmer for 15 minutes. Roast the garlic and onion in the cast iron pan for 15 minutes. Remove and peel the garlic; chop and measure 1/2 cup onion; reserve. Increase the heat to medium and roast the tomatillos for 10 minutes, making sure the skins darken.

In a food processor, place the cooked morita chiles, cooking liquid, garlic, onion, tomatillos, salt, smoked salt, brown sugar, and Chipotle Tabasco and process for 10 minutes. The pectin in the tomatillos will thicken the salsa. This salsa would traditionally be made in a molcajete. Yield 2 cups.

Serves 8
Heat level: **1 2 3 4 5 6 7** 8 9 10

Tip: *When you toast the chiles make sure to use the lowest setting so as not to scorch them. Scorching will result in a burnt acrid flavor, not the sweet smoky desirable flavor you want. Make sure to put the hood extractor on as you are toasting chiles, since the fumes can be intense.*

**You can substitute chipotles en adobo or another variety of dried chile in this recipe, adjusting the amount to your desired level of heat.*

Smoked Pimenton / SPAIN

Smoked chile powder from Spain is called Pimenton, and the best powders are from the town of La Vera in the Estremadura region of Spain. The idea of making paprika came from Spain, not Hungary, as most people believe. In Hungary, they do not dry the peppers for chile powder by smoking them but by hanging them out to dry in the air. In Spain, the sweet red chiles are picked in the early fall, and because the flesh of the chiles is too thick to dry outside in the air, the chiles are dried over smoky oak fires, resulting in the distinctive smoky sweet flavor that is the trademark of Pimenton and the secret scent that characterizes so much Spanish cuisine.

2 ounces chorizo picante, diced 1/8 inch (Palacio brand)
2 ounces sweet onion, diced 1/8 inch
2 cloves garlic, diced
1 tablespoon olive oil
1 tablespoon paprika, dulce (El Rey brand)
1 teaspoon paprika, picante (El Rey brand)
1/2 cup white wine
2 tablespoons sherry vinegar
1/2 teaspoon salt
1 clove garlic
12 ounces piquillo peppers* (Miguel and Valentino brand)
2 teaspoons tomato paste
1 tablespoon sherry (Oloroso brand)

Place the chorizo, onion, and diced garlic in a sauté pan. Add the olive oil, both paprikas, and the white wine and cook until the wine has evaporated. Add the sherry vinegar and let cook.

Place the salt on a cutting board and with the back of a chef's knife smash the clove garlic and mix with the salt to make a paste. Add to the cooked chorizo mixture. Cut the piquillo peppers in strips and add. Add the tomato paste and sherry and mix well. Yield 2 cups.

Serves 6
Heat level: 1 2 3 4 5 6 7 8 9 10

Tip: *There are three varieties of Spanish Pimenton: dulce, meaning sweet; agridulce, meaning half sweet, half smoky; and picante, meaning smoky and spicy. Buy all three and use them in different preparations. Look for Spanish Pimenton in grocery stores that specialize in imported Spanish products, like the Spanish Table (www.spanishtable.com), for the best choice and quality.*

**Fire roasted red bell peppers, peeled, deseeded, and cut in strips may be substituted.*

Chichilio Burnt Chile Salsa / OAXACA, MEXICO

There are many types of moles in Mexico that people should experience besides the classic model of dark brown mole from Oaxaca or Puebla that uses cocoa or chocolate as one of its ingredients. The word mole *means a sauce that contains a mixture of different chiles. There are red moles, green moles, black moles, yellow moles, and fruit moles. One of the most distinctive and definitely the smokiest is the chichilio mole of Oaxaca where dried chiles, avocado leaves, and dried tortillas are roasted until they are literally scorched. The first time I tasted this mole I thought it was going to taste like spicy, paste-like ashes. As I watched the cook prepare it from the beginning, I was sure she was going too far with her toasting or blackening of the ingredients. But I was wrong. Hundreds of years of tradition make this a great mole. Try it with roasted turkey or chicken enchiladas.*

15 cloves garlic
1 small onion
1/2 cup chopped tomato
1 1/2 ounces mulato chile, deseeded
1 1/2 ounces ancho chile, deseeded
1 1/2 ounces pasilla negro, deseeded
1 1/2 ounces guajillo chile, deseeded
1 1/2 ounces pasilla de Oaxaca or
morita chile, deseeded
8 cups water
4 prunes
2 teaspoons salt
1 1/2 teaspoons wild oregano, toasted
1 teaspoon cumin, toasted
1/4 teaspoon ground black pepper
2 tablespoons salsa de bruja (see page 180)

In a cast iron pan or comal heated to medium-low, roast the garlic and onion for 15 minutes. Chop and measure 1/2 cup onion; reserve. Over a fire on a grill, fire roast the tomato; reserve. Turn the cast iron pan or comal to medium-high heat and "burn" the chiles separately in batches until small spots of dark appear and the smoke starts to come from the chiles. This will indicate that the "burnt" flavoring technique is correct. Place the chiles in a medium saucepan and add 8 cups of water; add the prunes. Cook for 20 minutes on medium heat or until there is about 2 cups of liquid left. Place the chile mixture in a blender and add the salt, garlic and onion, and fire roasted tomato; puree. Crush the oregano with your fingers and add. Add the cumin, pepper, and salsa de bruja. Yield 3 cups.

Serves 8–10
Heat level: **1 2 3 4 5 6** 7 8 9 10

Pasilla de Oaxaca / MEXICO

Queen of all the chipotles, this chile is very rare but worthwhile to seek out. It offers richer, more complex smoky tones and is purer in flavor composition. Its name is a little confusing because a pasilla is the dark long chile of Central Mexico, and not related to this chile at all. This chile is only made in one village in Mexico outside of Oaxaca, so it is literally from only one village in the world. See sources (page 188) to order. It has a very strong smoky flavor that can perfume any soup, sauce, or salsa. Very captivating!

6 pasilla de Oaxaca chiles, dried
6 cups water
6 cloves garlic, smoked (see page 185)
3 tablespoons chopped onion
1 cup roasted cherry tomatoes (about 30)
3/4 teaspoon smoked salt
2 teaspoons tomato paste, double strength (365 brand)
1 teaspoon chipotle en adobo sauce
1 teaspoon brown sugar
1 teaspoon salsa de bruja* (see page 180)
1/4 teaspoon roasted and ground cumin
1/8 teaspoon ground allspice
1/8 teaspoon coriander
1 drop liquid smoke
1 tablespoon smoked chile oil (see page 93)

In a cast iron pan or comal heated to medium-low, toast the pasilla de Oaxaca chiles. Remove and place in a saucepan with seeds. Add 6 cups of water and reduce until 1 1/2 cups of liquid remain. Roast the garlic and onion for 15 minutes. Remove and reserve. Increase the temperature to medium-high and add the tomatoes and blacken. Place the chiles and the cooking liquid in a blender. Add the garlic, onion, tomatoes, smoked salt, tomato paste, chipotle en adobo sauce, brown sugar, salsa de bruja, cumin, allspice, coriander, and liquid smoke and puree. Top the salsa with smoked chile oil. Yield 2 cups.

Serves 8
Heat level: **1 2 3 4 5 6** 7 8 9 10

Tip: *To get more complexity in your cooking, use more than one type of chipotle or smoke flavor at a time in a recipe. Here I am using more than one type of chipotle—the dried pasilla de Oaxaca and the canned chipotle en adobo. The dried chile is more intense and gives the dish the desired rich smoky tone, and the canned chipotle adds a little sweetness and vinegar that make the salsa a little livelier.*

**Spicy herbal vinegar may be substituted.*

6 | Fresh and Easy Salsas

Hatch Green Chile Hummus and Zatar / CIRO

Robert and I came up with this salsa when I decided to throw a big Turkish party at my house. I had just returned from Istanbul and wanted to share with friends some of the wonderful flavors that I had discovered. Both Robert and I have wood burning ovens at our homes, but he is the maestro of the pizza oven. His fresh white truffle quail egg pizza, baked in 1 minute 40 seconds, is a masterpiece of creative flavors and traditional techniques. Turkey has wonderful pizzas, called pide, *or flatbreads. So, for appetizers, we decided to make pides from the oven and serve them with an assortment of olives and hummus and some other mezes. As it was August, New Mexican green chiles from Hatch New Mexico had just arrived in the markets, and they were fiery! Of course, I had to add them to the hummus. The hummus was a huge hit and everyone wanted the recipe, so here it is.*

1 1/4 cups garbanzo beans, dried, soaked*
6 cups water
1/2 small white onion
1 bay leaf
1 clove garlic
1 sprig thyme, wrapped in cheesecloth, tied
1/4 teaspoon salt
3/4 cup diced Hatch green chile (medium hot)
2 cloves garlic
1 tablespoon olive oil
1 tablespoon cured lemon peel
1 tablespoon lemon juice
6 tablespoons olive oil
1 teaspoon salt

Soak the garbanzo beans overnight in 2 cups water. Add 4 cups water and onion, bay leaf, garlic, and thyme; cover and simmer slowly over low heat for 1 hour. Uncover and cook for 15 minutes, letting the liquid evaporate. After 15 minutes check for softness. If more cooking is required, add more water if necessary. Add the salt at the end of cooking; there should be about 1/2 cup liquid left. This liquid helps to thin the garbanzo beans when pureed. Cover and let cool in the liquid.

Fire roast the green chile. Peel, deseed, and dice in small 1/8-inch pieces; reserve. Roast the 2 cloves garlic in a 400-degree-F oven in a clay pot roaster with olive oil for 40 minutes;

**1 can (25 ounces) Westbrae natural brand garbanzo beans (drained, rinsed, fast cooked) may be substituted. To fast cook the beans, use 1 1/2 cups water, onion, bay leaf, garlic, and thyme with drained garbanzo beans. Add salt if necessary.*

reserve. Remove any rind from the cured lemon and dice the peel fine; reserve. Place garbanzo beans (without liquid) in a food processor and add roasted garlic, lemon juice, olive oil, and salt. Puree until smooth. Use extra water if needed to thin. Remove from the processor. In a bowl, add the diced green chile and lemon peel to the hummus. Sprinkle with Zatar to serve. Yield 3 cups.

ZATAR

1 tablespoon coriander seeds
2 teaspoons cumin seeds
1 teaspoon fennel seeds
1/2 teaspoon anise seeds
1/2 teaspoon smoked salt
1/4 cup sesame seeds
4 teaspoons Aleppo chile flakes
1/4 teaspoon roasted ground black pepper
1 tablespoon sumac
2 tablespoons dried thyme

In a nonstick pan heated to medium-low, toast the coriander, cumin, fennel, and anise for 1 1/2 minutes. Place in a mortar and crush with smoked salt. Place the sesame seeds in the pan and toast for 2 minutes. Add Aleppo chile flakes and black pepper and continue to toast for 30 seconds. Add the sesame, chile flakes, and black pepper to the mortar and crush slightly. Add the sumac and thyme. Mix well.

Serves 6
Heat level: **1 2 3 4 5 6 7** 8 9 10

Pico de Gallo / MEXICO

The classic Mexican salsa, pico de gallo, has all the colors of the Mexican flag. Sometimes called salsa fresca, it is made with diced fresh, ripe, sweet tomatoes as an essential base, with aromatic cilantro, a touch of onion, and just the right amount of sharp green serrano chile to give it the right bite. The name of this salsa means "beak of the rooster" (or "peck of the rooster") and should provide the counterpoint or accent to something richer, whether it's an avocado salsa, carnitas taco, grilled skirt steak, or grilled fresh fish. The addition of a fresh element to a cooked dish is one of the elemental definitions of authentic Mexican cuisine.

2 tablespoons fine diced red or white onion
1 1/4 teaspoons salt
3/4 teaspoon superfine sugar or agave syrup
1 pound cherry tomatoes*
1 tablespoon fine minced serrano chiles, with seeds (about 3)
Zest of 1/2 lime (Microplaned)
1 tablespoon lime juice

Rinse the diced onion in cold water. Let dry and add salt and sugar. Slice the tomatoes into rings and add to onion mixture. Add the serrano chiles. (If you want the salsa less hot, reduce the amount of seeds added.) Add lime zest and juice. Let sit for 15 minutes. Yield 2 1/4 cups.

Serves 4
Heat level: **1 2 3 4 5 6** 7 8 9 10

Tip: *Use a light touch on the Microplane to get just the very thinnest essence of the lime zest without a touch of the pith. If you can see any white, you have gone down too far or are using too much pressure on the Microplane.*

Tip: *Add a touch of fructose sugar to the tomatoes to suggest sweeter, riper tomatoes.*

---

*Roma tomatoes diced in 3/8-inch pieces may be substituted.

Cherry Tomato Salsa Fresca with Basil / MEDITERRANEAN

For this salsa you need to find the best, sweetest, most intense cherry tomatoes. The best are usually the smallest ones that get fully ripe, have tender skins, and are sometimes called cherry 100s. A good brand is Texas Sweet. Homegrown cherry tomatoes are also wonderful. Some of the best tomatoes in the world are grown in Italy outside of Napoli. You can see them on long vines and strands sold in the markets or along the roadsides. The tomatoes are allowed to dry a little on the vine after fully ripening to bring up the percentage of sugar and evaporate some of the water. These are the famous San Marzano tomatoes that are the basis of the tomato sauce that goes on pizza and pasta. It is also worth experimenting with true Genovese basil if you have a small herb garden; it's easy to grow on a kitchen window box and a lot cheaper that the 6 leaves for $3.00 that you'll pay at a specialty market.

2 cups grape cherry tomatoes (about 12 ounces)
1/2 teaspoon salt
1/2 teaspoon sugar
2 teaspoons fine minced Fresno chiles, with seeds
1/2 lemon, zested (Microplaned)
1 teaspoon lemon juice
1 teaspoon lemon olive oil (Agrumato brand)*
4 teaspoons fine chiffonade basil, cut from small leaves
10 Lucques olives, pitted, rough chopped**

Slice the tomatoes thinly in rings and place in a mixing bowl. Sprinkle with the salt and sugar. Add the Fresno chiles with seeds. Add the lemon zest and juice. Add the lemon olive oil. Add the basil and olives. Yield 3 cups.

Serves 6
Heat level: **1 2 3** 4 5 6 7 8 9 10

**Use true lemon oil that is made from an olive oil pressed with lemons, not just a lemon oil extract added to inferior olive oil.*
***If you cannot get Lucques olives, I suggest any Italian green olive.*

Turkish Tomato Green Chile / TURKEY

Tomatoes are originally a New World plant and were brought back to Europe by the Spanish and Portuguese explorers, but it was in the exquisite Ottoman royal gardens that tomatoes were first featured as an ornamental plant. And it was from these gardens that the Italians first traded tomatoes back to Italy. They called it the Turkish fruit. Even today, some of the best tomatoes that you will ever eat are Turkish tomatoes, especially from the center of Turkey in the region of Cappadocia. The addition of the sumac powder to this dish gives it a beautiful Middle Eastern veil to wear.

1 1/2 pounds Roma tomatoes
1 clove garlic, sliced thin
1 teaspoon fine chopped thyme
1 teaspoon coriander
1/2 teaspoon cumin
2 teaspoons fructose or sugar
1 teaspoon salt
2 tablespoons sumac
2 tablespoons olive oil
1/2 cup chopped New Mexico Hatch green chile (medium hot)
1 tablespoon sumac
1/4 teaspoon salt
1 teaspoon cured lemon
3 tablespoons chopped Italian parsley
1 tablespoon lemon olive oil

Preheat oven to 200 degrees F. Prepare an ice bath and bring a large pot of water to a boil. Score an X on the bottom of each tomato and core. Plunge 4 tomatoes at a time into the boiling water for 10 to 15 seconds. Place directly in the ice bath. Repeat with the remaining tomatoes. Slip skins off and cut tomatoes in half.

Place the tomatoes in a bowl. Add the garlic, thyme, coriander, cumin, sugar, 1 teaspoon salt, 2 tablespoons sumac, and olive oil. Place tomatoes on a sheet pan lined with parchment paper or a Silpat, cut side down. Place in preheated oven and oven dry for 3 hours. Fire roast the green chile and place in a plastic bag to steam. When cool, peel, deseed, and fine chop. Place in a mixing bowl and add tomatoes that have been chopped. Add 1 tablespoon sumac, 1/4 teaspoon salt, cured lemon, parsley, and lemon olive oil. Yield 3 cups.

Serves 8
Heat level: **1 2 3 4** 5 6 7 8 9 10

Tip: *You can buy preserved lemon in the olive departments of Whole Foods or from the Spanish Table or any good Middle Eastern grocery store. Or you can make your own (see page 188).*

Fire Roasted Hatch Green Chile Salsa / NEW MEXICO

You can tell when green chile season starts in Santa Fe, New Mexico: if you are driving down Cerrilos Road and smell that unique charred hot sweet smell coming from the propane chile roasters, you know it's starting. I am lucky enough to live in Santa Fe where we can buy green chiles in bushel bags at the grocery store, take them outside to the parking lot and get them roasted for $2.00, and then take them home, skin them, and put them in freezer bags—after a tasty sampling of a few first, of course! Green chiles are delicious simply wrapped in a fresh corn tortilla and roasted over an open flame. You should only try to make this salsa if you can find fresh green chiles to roast. You could also make this salsa with a combination of jalapeños and poblanos if you want.

1/2 teaspoon Mexican oregano
1 pound New Mexico Hatch green chiles (hot)
4 cloves garlic
2 tablespoons fine chopped white onion
1 1/4 teaspoons salt
2 tablespoons unseasoned rice wine vinegar (Marukan brand)
1/2 teaspoon green pepper Tabasco

Toast the oregano in a nonstick sauté pan over low heat for 2 minutes. Let cool; reserve. Over a flame, place a grilling grate and toast the Hatch chiles, blistering the skins, then place in a plastic bag to steam. Peel and deseed when cool; reserve. In a cast iron pan or comal heated to medium-low, roast the garlic and onion slowly for 15 minutes. When cool, make a paste with the salt and garlic and place in a food processor. Put in the green chiles, onion, rice wine vinegar, and green pepper Tabasco. Pulse until a smooth spread is achieved. Using your fingers, crush the reserved oregano into the salsa. Yield 2 cups.

Serves 6
Heat level: **1 2 3 4 5 6** 7 8 9 10

Tip: *It's very important when roasting chiles of any type that you do not wash them under running water when cleaning them, as you will lose all the chile "oil" and most of the roasted flavor. Just use the backside of a knife and a clean cloth. You have to clean them while they are still warm, otherwise they get into a soggy mush and you can't get rid of the stem seeds and charred skins. Unfortunately, most factory-produced green chile is usually washed.*

Padron / SPAIN

The padron chile, also known as "pimento de padron" in Spanish, is a small green chile named after the town of Padron, Spain. A favorite all over Spain, in the late summer and early fall this chile shows up in almost every tapas bar. Huge piles of the small, intense green chiles are quickly flash fried in virgin olive oil and sprinkled with sea salt, then rushed to the bar to be consumed along with cold cana (small draft beers) or glasses of refreshing cool wine. The chiles are eaten hot and whole, except for the stem, and the fun and bravado is to find the ones that are seriously hot from among the plate—a sort of "chile roulette"! These chiles have a fresh, sweet flavor that goes well with a big grilled steak, on a pizza, or thrown in a salad.

1/3 cup Spanish olive oil
4 cloves garlic, sliced thin
4 tablespoons capers in white balsamic, drained
2 teaspoons whole thyme, stems removed
60 padron peppers*
2 teaspoons Spanish olive oil
1 teaspoon diced cured lemon
1/2 teaspoon coarse sea salt

In a 12-inch sauté pan over medium heat, add 1/3 cup olive oil and fry the garlic until golden brown. Remove to a paper towel to drain. Fry the capers for 1 minute. Remove to a paper towel to drain. Fry the thyme for 1 minute. Remove to a paper towel to drain. Fry the padron peppers until the skins blister. When cool, cut off the stems and push the seeds out. (This process is similar to pushing toothpaste from the bottom of the tube.) Cut the peppers in 1/2-inch strips and layer on a plate. Place the garlic as the next layer, then capers. Sprinkle with 2 teaspoons olive oil, cured lemon, and coarse salt. Yield 2 1/2 cups.

Serves 8
Heat level: **1 2 3** 4 5 6 7 8 9 10

**Choose same size peppers for equal cooking.*

Raita / INDIA

Whenever you find strong, intensely spiced foods you usually find a salsa next to them. As interesting as strongly spiced foods are, sometimes you need to create a little "palate space"—between bites, between different spiced dishes on the same plate, or just to cleanse the palate. Nowhere is this truer than in Indian cuisine. The palate-cleansing salsa can be a yogurt raita, a sweet chutney, or a sour green mango pickle. This recipe makes one of the most interesting raita that I have ever had, and it uses one of the world's most unusual chiles—the sun-dried yogurt chile from India. It is available online at www.kalustyans.com. It's also important to use really good natural yogurt for the salsa base; the Greek style creamy yogurt or the Bulgarian natural ones are usually the best to look for. Use this raita with all types of grilled Indian breads (like nans), on falafels, or as an interesting dip for dolmas.

3/4 teaspoon kosher salt
3 tablespoons minced shallot
1 cup grated English or Persian cucumber
Zest of 1/2 Meyer lemon
1 tablespoon Meyer lemon juice
2 cups plain whole milk yogurt
2 teaspoons lemon olive oil
2 tablespoons fine julienne mint
2 tablespoons fine julienne cilantro
3/8 teaspoon anise seeds
3/8 teaspoon coriander seeds
1/4 teaspoon cumin seeds
3/8 teaspoon cayenne
1 ounce sun-dried yogurt curd chiles (Kalustyan's)

Place the salt in a bowl and add the minced shallot. Grate the cucumber on the finest blade of a Benriner, or Japanese mandoline, and add to the shallots. Let sit for 10 minutes. The shallot and cucumber mixture will give off water. Remove excess water for a thicker salsa and less harsh shallot taste. Add the lemon zest, lemon juice, yogurt, lemon olive oil, mint, and cilantro. Grind all the seeds in a spice mill or mortar. In a sauté pan heated to low, toast the anise, coriander, cumin, and cayenne; while still warm add to the yogurt. Seed the chiles and cut in thin strips. Top the salsa with the chile strips. Yield 3 cups.

Serves 6
Heat level: **1 2 3** 4 5 6 7 8 9 10

FINE SPECIALTY FOODS
CURD CHILE
PRODUCT OF INDIA
HEAT SCALE: 3 OUT OF 10

Ripe Tomato, Thai Basil / THAILAND

Another of my own invented simple "International Salsa Frescas," this salsa pairs the sweet base of ripe cherry tomatoes against the accent of piquant Thai green chiles and all the perfumes of the Thai aromatics: lemongrass, kaffir lime, lime zest, Thai basil. It changes the whole idea of ordinary salsa fresca into a garden of captivating aromas. The Southeast Asian cuisines excel in the use of aromatics like no other in the world. A Vietnamese market looks like a garden shop on steroids, with bouquets of herbs the size of bouquets of a dozen roses. Herbs make dishes healthier and create layers of experience within a dish. Use this salsa for Thai beef salad or as a salsa for seafood or grilled shrimp. It's great on Thai shrimp tacos, too.

2 cups cherry tomatoes
2 Thai chiles
1 teaspoon fine minced lemongrass
1/4 teaspoon finest julienne kaffir lime leaf
1/2 teaspoon salt
2 teaspoons sugar
1/4 teaspoon lime zest*
1 teaspoon lime juice*
1 teaspoon fine minced shallot
2 tablespoons finest julienne Thai basil
1 teaspoon fish sauce (3 Crabs brand)

Slice the cherry tomatoes in rings and place in a bowl. Slice the Thai chiles in rings and add to the tomatoes. Add the lemongrass, kaffir lime leaf, salt, sugar, lime zest, lime juice, shallot, Thai basil, and fish sauce. Yield 2 1/4 cups.

Serves 4

Heat level: **1 2 3 4 5 6 7** 8 9 10

Tip: *When you buy fish sauce, buy it only from an Asian market that has a good turnover of products and look for the lightest colored ones as they get darker when they age. After opening, put a date on the bottle and refrigerate; throw away after 60 days, otherwise the fish sauce is too strong and "fishy" tasting. Fish sauce should provide a light fermented or umami accent to the dish, not ruin the dish with an overpowering "fishy" flavor. The reason most people don't like fish sauce is that they have never tasted good, fresh fish sauce.*

**Use kaffir lime if available.*

Fire Engine Red Salsa / MEXICO

Fun, fast, and fiery! And did I mention smoky? This salsa takes its name from the red Fresno chile, a real favorite of mine. Often mislabeled in produce departments or cookbooks as a green jalapeño, the red Fresno does look like a jalapeño in overall shape. But the flavor of the Fresno is quite a bit different than that of its sharper cousin. The Fresno (named after Fresno, California, a town in the Central Valley of California at the center of huge agricultural farms) is both sweeter and hotter than a jalapeño. It has the natural ripened sweetness of a sweet red bell pepper with a distinct "heat," without any of the "veggie" tones of a green bell pepper or jalapeño. I often use this chile sliced in rings as a garnish for Asian dishes, especially if I cannot find, or if I want, something a little milder than the blistering Thai chiles.

10 cloves garlic
1 cup diced white onion (about 1 large)
24 Fresno chiles
1 can (28 ounces) fire roasted tomatoes* (Muir Glen brand)
1 teaspoon salt
1/2 teaspoon smoked salt
1 teaspoon white balsamic vinegar**
1 teaspoon adobo sauce from chipotle en adobo

In a cast iron pan or comal over medium-low heat, dry roast the garlic and onion for 15 minutes. Over a medium flame on a grill, fire roast the Fresnos, then remove the stems when cool. Keep the burnt skins on. In a blender, add the garlic, onion, Fresnos, tomatoes, salt, smoked salt, balsamic vinegar, and adobo sauce and blend until chunky. Yield 3 cups.

Serves 8
Heat level: 1 2 3 4 5 6 7 8 9 10

**This salsa uses canned tomatoes that are fire roasted, which is a recent welcome arrival to the grocery aisle. It makes the job of finding ripe tomatoes and fire roasting them for a recipe a lot easier.*
***White balsamic vinegar is a great addition to your pantry arsenal. Lighter than regular balsamic, it provides just the right "pick me up" to this dish to make it "zing" a little more. Anytime you add an acid—whether it's a vinegar or citrus juice—to a salsa, it dissolves some of the capsaicin, the chemical in the chile that makes it hot, which spreads the heat around a bit in the dish.*

Tomatillo Avocado Salsa / MEXICO

Tomatillo Avocado Salsa is one of the workhorse salsas of my cantina kitchen. It seems to be everyone's favorite, whether it's dribbled on tacos pastor or used as a side dip for chips. This velvety, bright green salsa has just the right balance of acidic fruit, aromatic cilantro, and cooling, rich avocado. More dynamic in taste than regular guacamole, and a lot easier to hold for long periods of time without it turning brown, this is definitely one of the top three salsas that you need for a Mexican kitchen or Mexican party.

12 ounces tomatillos
2 tablespoons chopped white onion
1 1/2 serrano chiles, rough chopped, with seeds
1/3 cup tightly packed cilantro
3/4 teaspoon salt
3/4 teaspoon sugar
2 teaspoons lime juice
2 avocados, peeled and pitted
4 tablespoons ice

Wash the tomatillos in hot water 5 to 10 times until there is no foam coming from the water. This removes the bitterness. Heat a large pot of water to a boil and prepare an ice bath. Boil the tomatillos and onion for 4 minutes, then shock in ice water. Remove from the ice water and place the cooled tomatillo and onion in a blender. Add serrano chiles, cilantro, salt, sugar, lime juice, avocado, and ice cubes. Blend 2 minutes or until smooth. Yield 2 cups.

Serves 6
Heat level: **1 2 3 4** 5 6 7 8 9 10

Tip: *The real trick to making this salsa is to buy the right tomatillos. Look for tomatillos that have clean outside skins, not too dark or spotted. The tomatillos should be very dark green—kelly green not lime green. They should be very firm. Buy smaller ones rather than the huge ones that you see in all the national chains, or at least buy tomatillos that all match in size so that they cook at the same rate. The tomatillos have to be washed very thoroughly and repeatedly in very hot water or the salsa will be bitter.*

Zhug / CIRO

My first taste of this intriguing, complex salsa was memorable. Walking through an older small market in Jerusalem and tasting everything that looked great, I came across a fabulous falafel cart. The vendor was piling the crispy falafel balls into a huge freshly stuffed whole-wheat flour pita on a bed of lettuce, tomatoes, and hummus, and then you could choose any of fifteen salsas and pickles to top your falafel. I immediately went about tasting each and every one. The zhug stood out because it was captivating and I could not figure out all the flavors right away; I don't think I had ever come across quite the same combination of flavors before. The salsa traces its origins back to the days of Arabian traders in Yemen, and it's the Jewish settlers from Yemen who brought this taste back to Israel. This popular Yemenite hot salsa is a sort of Middle Eastern chimichurri, is also called "skhug" and comes in two forms, red and green.

2 cloves garlic
1 3/4 teaspoons salt
1/4 cup Meyer lemon, zested, juiced (about 2 small)
2 tablespoons pickled jalapeño juice (La Costeña brand)
2/3 cup diced cucumber
5 tablespoons diced green bell pepper
3/4 cup stemmed and chopped Italian parsley
1/2 cup chopped basil or cilantro
1 tablespoon chopped tarragon
1 tablespoon chopped fennel fronds or mint
2 tablespoons fine diced jalapeño, without seeds
1 tablespoon lemon olive oil
1 tablespoon olive oil
1 teaspoon chile caribe
1/3 cup diced cucumber

Peel the garlic and mash it with the salt. Place the lemon juice in a blender. Add the zest, jalapeño juice, 2/3 cup diced cucumber, green bell pepper, and mashed garlic. Puree for 2 minutes on low speed. Place in a mixing bowl. Add the parsley, basil or cilantro, tarragon, and fennel fronds or mint. Add the jalapeño, lemon olive oil, olive oil, and chile caribe. Stir in 1/3 cup diced cucumber. Yield 2 cups.

Serves 8
Heat level: **1 2 3 4 5 6 7** 8 9 10

Rocoto / PERU

Rocoto chiles are deep red or orange and shaped like a very large habanero chile, about 3 inches long by 2 1/2 inches, elongated, and thick fleshed with black seeds. I find them to be bitter and a bit tannic, so I usually rinse them under cold water after soaking them. This also washes away some of the heat to make the chiles more manageable. Blood orange juice has the perfect color, acidity, and fruit flavor to combine with rocoto chiles. Use them together in salsas or ceviches. Rocoto chiles are becoming more popular as Peruvian seafood (which uses plenty of rocoto chiles) has taken the gourmet restaurant world by storm.

1 cup vinegar (Heinz brand)
1 teaspoon sugar
1 tablespoon sea salt
2 ounces rocoto chile peppers
1 tablespoon olive oil
1 ounce rocoto chile peppers
1 clove garlic
1 bell pepper, diced
1 large Roma tomato, diced
1 cup water
1 teaspoon sea salt
2 tablespoons blood orange juice

Place the vinegar in a bowl with the sugar and 1 tablespoon salt. Cut, deseed, and place 2 ounces of rocoto peppers in the bowl and let sit for 10 minutes. Rinse the rocotos under cold water 2 times.

Place the olive oil in a sauté pan and add the rinsed rocotos, the plain rocoto that has not been rinsed, the garlic, and bell pepper and sauté for 6 minutes over medium heat. Add the tomato, water, and 1 teaspoon salt and cook for 4 more minutes. When cool, place in a blender and add the blood orange juice. Blend until smooth. Yield 1 1/2 cups.

Serves 8
Heat level: **1 2 3 4 5 6 7 8 9** 10

Hatchamole / NEW MEXICO

Two of my favorite foods combined into one great dish: the unique flavor of the ripe, roasted New Mexican green chile—arguably the best green chile in the world—paired with ripe, silken, rich avocado flesh is a magical culinary marriage. The depth and length of the flavor profile of the roasted green chile creates a more mature guacamole. It has a more complex character than the regular fresher model. Use this salsa on quesadillas, roasted sea bass, or grilled hamburgers. Every year New Mexico has a contest for the best green chile burger in the state—this would make a great green chile burger!

1/2 cup fine diced Hatch green chiles
1 tablespoon minced green onion, white part only
2 tablespoons lime juice
1 teaspoon salt
1 pound avocados
1/4 cup cilantro
1 teaspoon green pepper Tabasco

Fire roast the Hatch chiles, blistering the skin. Place in a plastic bag to steam. When cool, peel, deseed, and dice fine. Reserve. In a molcajete, place the minced onion, lime juice, and salt. Let sit for 10 minutes. Add the avocado pulp and mash. Add the green chile, cilantro, and green pepper Tabasco. Yield 2 1/2 cups.

Serves 6
Heat level: **1 2 3 4 5 6 7** 8 9 10

Tip: *The New Mexican green chile is only valuable fresh for about 2 months per year, from about early August to early October. The other green chile that you see sold all year long is the Anaheim green chile grown in California, which does not have the same flavor at all. I suggest you buy green chiles online during the fresh season. For example, the central market in Texas has a huge green chile promotion every year. Or go to the Web to find a green chile shipper from Hatch, New Mexico, where some of the best green chiles are grown. Hatch New Mexico green chiles taste different because they are grown at higher altitudes (over 4,000 feet) so the plants get different sunlight (more ultraviolet), which is good for chiles. The soil is also more alkaline.*

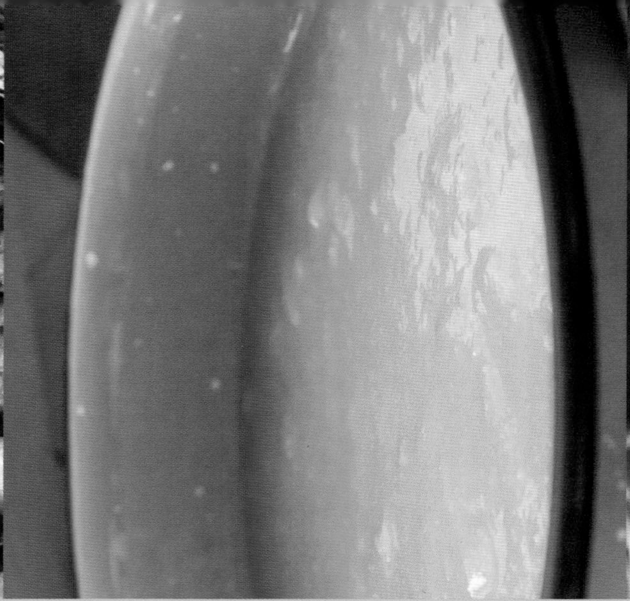

7 | Fireworks Salsas

Laos Charred Eggplant / LAOS

I remember the first time I had this salsa about fifteen years ago; it was on the terrace of a Thai restaurant of the Four Seasons in Chiang Mai (then called the Regent) overlooking lush verdant rice fields below. It was on a warm evening, and I ordered some cooling cocktails. They brought out roasted cashews that were spiced with kaffir lime leaf, still warm, and a roasted eggplant dip with fresh, crispy shrimp chips. I loaded a chip with the eggplant salsa and was immediately assaulted with a range of intense, smoky, fiery, savory, and aromatic essences wrapped in a velvety texture on this crunchy, feather-light, salty, pungent chip. It was truly one of the most remarkable taste sensations of all time. Charred Eggplant salsa is often sold next to vendors that make and grill Chiang Mai sausages—the salsa is perfect as a side dish at any southeast Asian meal or as a side for grilled pork or chicken. By itself it makes a great dip.

9 ounces Chinese eggplant (about 4)
6 ounces Hatch green chile, hot variety (about 5)
4 cloves garlic
2 small shallots, sliced into 1/8-inch rings
8 Thai green chiles
1/2 teaspoon smoked salt
1/2 teaspoon kosher salt
1/2 teaspoon sugar
1 tablespoon fish sauce (3 Crabs brand)
1 teaspoon lime juice
2 tablespoons rough chopped cilantro

Preheat oven to 350 degrees F. Place a grill basket over a high flame and grill the eggplant for 5 to 6 minutes on all sides, making sure to char all the skin completely. Place eggplant in the oven for 10 minutes. Remove eggplant from oven and let cool before peeling.

Grill the Hatch green chile until all the skin has been charred and then place in a plastic bag to steam for 10 minutes. Peel and deseed the chile with the back of a knife. Make a paste by mashing the chile and add to peeled eggplant.

Heat a cast iron pan over medium-low heat and roast the garlic, shallots, and Thai chiles for 12 minutes, turning often. Place the garlic, shallots, and chiles in a mortar and add smoked salt, kosher salt, and sugar. With a pestle make a paste. Add the eggplant mixture, fish sauce, lime juice, and cilantro. Serve with fried shrimp chips. Yield 2 cups.

Serves 4
Heat level: **1 2 3 4 5 6 7 8 9** 10

Tip: *Try to use the Asian eggplants, Chinese or Japanese, as they are less bitter and have a higher proportion of skin to flesh so you get more charred flavor and they are easier to cook all the way through.*

Net 24 Fl.Oz. (1Pt.4 Fl.Oz.) 682ml
FDA REGISTRATION NO. 10757642294

Sriracha / THAILAND

Sriracha has become the modern ketchup—ketchup with an "edge." You see the plastic squeeze bottle with the Vietnamese writing everywhere. Originally a spicy red chile salsa made in southern Thailand, it became popular with the Vietnamese pho houses that serve it to accompany the bowls of steaming pho, along with hoisin sauce. Now I see Sriracha at hot dog stands, taco stands, hamburger bars, and as a topping for French fries. It is fairly easy to make—just a simple fermented product—and will last in the fridge for quite a while, so it's worth making your own since most commercial varieties have lots of preservatives and are often loaded with MSG. You can also make this salsa from hot New Mexican red chiles when they are available in the late fall after they turn red, but only for a short time. They do make a superior salsa.

1 pound Fresno chiles
2 cloves garlic
2 tablespoons salt
3 tablespoons sugar
3 tablespoons white vinegar (Heinz brand)
2 tablets acidophilus, crushed

Cut the stems off the Fresno chiles. Peel the garlic and place in a food processor with the chiles. Add the salt, sugar, vinegar, and crushed acidophilus. Puree to a fine paste. Put the puree in a bowl and cover with a cheesecloth; let sit out for 24 hours. In a blender, puree mixture and strain through a medium mesh strainer until seeds are removed. The salsa is now ready but must be refrigerated. Yield 1 2/3 cups.

Serves 8
Heat level: **1 2 3 4 5 6 7 8** 9 10

Note: *The Fresno chile is a red chile that is often mistakenly called a red jalapeño. It is the same size but is a different species of chile.*

Mango Habanero / SOUTH AMERICA

This is a wonderful, simple salsa that is bright, fiery, and fruity. Roasted Habanero and Mango is a real favorite of mine that I can make in a few minutes. Habaneros are not only hot and colorful, but have a great tropical, fruity flavor. Whenever I am making a tropical meal from the southern part of Mexico or the Caribbean, I instinctively use habanero chiles, usually in a number of places. A ripe habanero has the perfume of ripe pineapple and citrus and pairs wonderfully with all the other tropical fruits. To further bring out that tropical perfume, you need to slowly dry roast the habanero over low heat, until it has become soft but not blackened. After you roast the habanero, slice it open. Pick it up with a fork and smell the fruity scent compared to a raw one. The aroma is like a tropical fruit garden. With tropical salsas, always try to use fresh limes that are ripe; the natural acidity balances the sweetness of very ripe fruits. Key limes are better still as they have even more perfume than regular Persian limes. This salsa is fantastic for seafood tacos, grilled chicken, crab tostadas, and tropical tortas.

4 habanero chiles
2 mangos
2 tablespoons sugar
3 tablespoons lime juice
1/8 teaspoon salt
2 teaspoons rice wine vinegar (Maruka brand)
2 sweet hot pickled habaneros
1 teaspoon sweet hot pickled habanero syrup

In a cast iron pan or comal heated to medium-low, roast the habaneros for 12 minutes, turning often. Remove the seeds and place chiles in a blender. Peel the mango and cut lengthwise along the pit and remove the fruit. Then on a grater on the biggest grate, grate against the mango pit, removing any pulp (or use the back of a knife to release the pulp). Place in the blender and add sugar, lime juice, salt, vinegar, pickled habaneros, and the syrup from the pickled habaneros. Blend until smooth. Yield 2 cups.

Serves 8
Heat level: **1 2 3 4 5 6 7 8** 9 10

Tip: *When you buy pickled habaneros, save the juice in the jar for salsa or make sure to put some of the pickling juice in the container if you take out pickled habaneros from the olive bars where they are usually sold in grocery stores.*

Habanero Hot Dog Relish / BAHAMAS

I grew up in New England, which has a lengthy, gray, grave, cold winter during which you anxiously develop a pent-up demand for sunshine and warm weather and the glorious fun foods of summer. Starting on Memorial Day, we reveled with grilled hot dogs (with relish and mustard), late night black raspberry ice cream at the dairy hops, fried clam rolls, juicy hamburgers, frappés (New England jargon for "milkshakes"), and frozen Milky Way bars at the lake. And from those days, grilled hot dogs with all the toppings are still an emotional favorite of mine. I still search out a great grilled "dog" on the streets of Berlin or Bangkok, usually after some late-night revelry and a few drinks. A great dog needs a great relish, and this is one. It also goes well with burgers and tacos.

1/2 cup thin sliced cippolini onions
5 Fresno chiles
5 habanero chiles (sliced in strips)
2 habanero chiles (sliced in rings)
1/2 cup sliced carrots
1 teaspoon fresh grated turmeric*
2 cups white vinegar (Heinz brand)
3/4 cup sugar
1 teaspoon salt
1 teaspoon sweet hot mustard (Inglehoffer brand)
1 clove
1 allspice berry
1/2 teaspoon dill seed

Blanch the onions in salted, boiling water. Then place in a medium saucepan. Devein and deseed the Fresnos and 5 habaneros; slice in strips. Add to the pan. Cut the 2 habaneros in rings with seeds. Add to the pan. On a mandoline, cut the carrots in matchsticks. Add to the pan. Grate the turmeric and add to the pan. Add the vinegar, sugar, salt, mustard, clove, and allspice and cook for 20 minutes. Add the dill seed at the end of cooking. Yield 2 cups.

Serves 8
Heat level: **1 2 3 4 5 6 7 8** 9 10

Tip: *To make it even more fiery, use this relish on hot links from Louisiana, hot Andouille sausages, or green chile sausages.*

**1/2 teaspoon dry turmeric may be substituted.*

SWEET HOT MUSTARD

Serrano Green Tomato Salsa / MEXICO

This recipe is inspired by the classic salsa verde of Mexico that uses tomatillos for its base. Here I am using ripe green tomatoes with roasted, sizzling serrano chiles. Fresh basil and tarragon are added to create a delightful herbal accent that goes well with cold salads, pastas, and seafood. Green tomatoes, which you can find in the summertime, are sometimes called green zebra tomatoes. A green tomato is not just an unripe red tomato and it has a different flavor and acidity from red tomatoes. If you cannot find green tomatoes, I suggest you use tomatillos, which are available all year long; they work great. Do not overblend the salsa as you will get too much air into it and that will affect the "mouth feel" and flavor intensity. This salsa should be silky and velvety and very bright green.

8 serrano chiles
1 teaspoon sugar
1 teaspoon lime juice
1 tablespoon minced white onion
1/2 clove garlic
1 teaspoon salt
2 cups rough chopped green tomato
4 basil leaves
1 tablespoon tarragon
2 teaspoons olive oil

In a cast iron pan or comal over medium heat, roast the serrano chiles. When cool, peel and put in a blender with the seeds. In a bowl, add the sugar and lime juice. Rinse the onion in cold water and add to the bowl; let sit for 10 minutes. Mash the garlic with the salt to make a paste. Add to the blender. Add the onion mixture and green tomato, basil, and tarragon. Pulse for 1 minute to obtain a rough chopped salsa. Stir in the olive oil. Yield 2 cups.

Serves 6
Heat level: **1 2 3 4 5 6 7 8** 9 10

Tip: *If you want even more blistering to the tongue, use green habanero chiles or green Scotch bonnet chiles and leave some of the seeds in.*

Dog Snout Salsa (Ixnepech) / MAYAN

This salsa is named after a dog's snout, which is usually wet and running; and this salsa will turn your nose into a running wet snout, guaranteed! The profuse use of extra hot chiles gives this salsa an intensity that is a long way from salsa fresca. Almost an extreme salsa, it picks up the faintest dishes to give them spirit. The combination of juices here mimics the flavor of the sour orange that we do not have readily available; also the acidity of the juices brings out the capsaicin to make the salsa hotter. Any time you add salt, vinegar, acid, or alcohol to a dish with chiles, it gets hotter as the capsaicin dissolves with these ingredients. Dog Snout Salsa is very colorful, with the bright orange cherry tomatoes and red chiles. It's great for taco parties or for extreme salsa dip and goes well with all the fast and furious sports.

1 dried habanero chile
5 tablespoons sour orange juice*
1/4 cup fine diced red onion, rinsed in cold water
1 1/4 teaspoons salt
4 roasted habaneros, minced
1 1/2 cups orange cherry tomatoes, diced fine
3 tablespoons fine chopped cilantro

In a cast iron pan or comal over medium-low heat, toast the dry habanero. Remove from heat and grind in a mortar. Reserve 1 teaspoon; save the rest for another use. Place the sour orange juice in a bowl. Add the onion and salt. Let sit for 10 minutes.

Roast the habaneros over medium heat in the cast iron pan for 8 minutes, turning occasionally.

Mince the habaneros, without seeds. To the bowl with the sour orange juice, add the diced tomatoes, minced habaneros, cilantro, and reserved teaspoon of ground dried habanero. Yield 2 cups.

Serves 8
Heat level: **1 2 3 4 5 6 7 8 9 10**

**To make sour orange juice, combine 4 tablespoons orange juice, 1 tablespoon grapefruit juice, and 1 tablespoon lemon juice.*

Amarillo Yellow Tomato Guerro / MEXICO

The light pale yellow chile called the guerro is featured here. The word guerro *in Spanish is from the word "blond," and the chiles are the size and shape of a jalapeño. It has some heat but an overall mild flavor. This chile is used extensively in pickling dishes or escabeches. The recipe mixes the guerro chile with its hotter cousin, the habanero, and is then blended with roasted fruit to create a salsa that has depth and bright fire. The colorful orange bell peppers give it a richer hue. You could also add red bell peppers if you cannot find orange bell peppers. The ingredients are not cooked together and cooked down as they would be for a mole, so the layering of flavors is more distinct.*

1 white onion, peeled, cut in half
2 cloves garlic
2 habaneros, cut in half, with seeds
1 tablespoon olive oil
6 guerro chiles
2 pounds yellow tomatoes, cored
1 orange bell pepper, stemmed, seeded, rough chopped
1/2 golden pineapple, cored
1 teaspoon salt
1 teaspoon sugar
1/2 teaspoon white balsamic
1 teaspoon white vinegar

Preheat oven to 450 degrees F. Put the onion, garlic, and habaneros on a sheet of parchment paper. Add the olive oil. Fold the paper in half, creating a pyramid shape by folding the edges starting from one end continuing to the opposite end; fold each fold over the last fold to create a seal, finishing by tucking the end fold under the parcel. Bake this papillote for 30 minutes. (This can be made with tinfoil as well.)

Place the guerro chiles, tomatoes, and bell pepper in a baking casserole dish and bake for 40 minutes, uncovered. On a half sheet pan, oven roast the 1/2 pineapple for 40 minutes.

Place the onion, garlic, and habaneros in a blender. Add the guerro chiles, tomatoes, bell pepper, and roasted pineapple. Blend and finish with salt, sugar, white balsamic, and vinegar. Yield 4 cups.

Serves 12
Heat level: **1 2 3 4 5 6 7** 8 9 10

Tip: *This recipe calls for white balsamic vinegar, which has a more subtle, gentler vinegar profile with a delicate light touch than regular balsamic vinegar. It is readily available in the vinegar section.*

Szechuan Eggplant / CHINA

When you say or think of the word Szechuan, the first thing that comes to mind is chiles. This fiery cuisine with its star flavor of chiles captivates its audience; it awakens the senses and stimulates the soul. The capital of Szechuan is Chengdu, and it is here that you are in chile heaven or chile hell, depending upon your inclinations. In Chengdu, chiles cover the food; you have to dig through mounds of fried chiles to find morsels of meat in famous dishes, like "bone and chiles," which is literally fried pork neck bones with large blanket of red chiles. In hot pots, the chiles cover the surface so thickly that you cannot see the broth or the oil; in Mapo Dofu you cannot see the tofu. In Szechuan, the chile is the reason to eat the dish, not the accessory.

1 pound Japanese eggplant
1 teaspoon kosher salt
2 cups peanut oil, for frying
1 red bell pepper
4 whole Arbol chiles
1/4 cup diagonally sliced green onion
1/2 cup diced celery heart and leaves
1 1/4 teaspoons ground Szechuan peppercorns
1/2 teaspoon chile oil (page 93)
2 teaspoons sweet soy sauce
1 tablespoon black vinegar
1/2 teaspoon salt
1/2 teaspoon sugar
1 tablespoon tangerine juice

Dice the eggplant in 1/4-inch pieces (leaving skin on) and sprinkle with salt. Place in a colander and put a plate on top of the eggplant with a weight to let water release for 1 hour.

In a deep-sided pan, heat the peanut oil to 350 degrees F and oil roast the bell pepper. Place in a plastic bag to steam. When cool, peel, deseed, and dice. Measure 1/2 cup of bell pepper and put in a mixing bowl.

Place the eggplant on a paper towel to remove any excess water. Turn the oil heat up to 375 degrees F and oil roast the diced eggplant for 2 minutes. Remove from oil and place on paper towels to absorb any excess oil. Place in the bowl.

Fry the Arbol chiles for 1 minute or less to intensify the capsicum. Flake the chile in a spice mill and add to the bowl. Add the green onion and celery. Add the ground Szechuan peppercorns, chile oil, sweet soy sauce, black vinegar, salt, sugar, and tangerine juice. Yield 2 1/2 cups.

Serves 6

Heat level: **1 2 3 4 5 6 7 8** 9 10

Tip: *Look for the long Chinese celery at Asian grocery stores; it has more green leaves and much thinner stalks than the grocery celery that is often missing its leaves.*

Chiu Chow Chile Oil / CHINA

This is a powerful salsa from southern China. The Chiu Chow chile oil is usually sold in a bottle in the vast display of chile pastes and seasoning in large Asian grocery stores. The paste contains the chile part and the oil has the flavor (usually the Lee Kim Keep Brand is the best). It is basically roasted garlic chile oil, but for this recipe I have added a number of divergent regional products together that you would not see together traditionally but that work well. The resulting salsa is much more layered and complex, and fresher. It does have a lot of ingredients, but is really unique and will be the talk of the party. The technique of making a quick, light pickle gives the dish a much lighter and more modern sensibility. Most of the traditional dishes in China were made for preserving and using over the long winter months when no fresh vegetables were available. Traditionally, the picking is quite strong and salty. I prefer a gentler touch in my food, and less salt, but still enjoy the complexity that pickling gives a dish.

1/3 cup roasted garlic, peeled (about 15 cloves)
1 tablespoon toasted sesame oil
4 tablespoons ground Arbol chile (about 24 chiles)
1 cup soybean oil
3 tablespoons organic soy (Kikkoman brand)
1 tablespoon toasted sesame oil
1 teaspoon fine ground salt
1 teaspoon honey

Oven roast the garlic in a covered pan with 1 tablespoon sesame oil for 40 minutes at 375 degrees F. Mash the garlic; reserve. Grind the Arbol chiles in a spice mill to flakes (larger pieces are preferred) and place in a stainless steel bowl. Heat the soybean oil to 375 degrees F and immediately, while the oil is still hot, add the mashed garlic and then pour over the chiles. Let the oil cool. Add the soy, 1 tablespoon sesame oil, salt, and honey. Mix well. Yield 1 1/2 cups.

Serves 12
Heat level: **1 2 3 4 5 6 7 8** 9 10

Nouc Cham / VIETNAM

This is the most famous salsa of Vietnam; you see it on all the tables at Vietnamese and Asian restaurants. It's served with famous Vietnamese spring rolls and often with the cold noodle dishes that come with grilled pork, Bunn dishes, and other Vietnamese delicacies that are wrapped and rolled. Vietnamese food is very aromatic with lots of raw strong herbs, such as mint, cilantro, sesame leaf, lemongrass, basil, and sawtooth. It often needs this savory accompaniment to round out the flavors and provide the right amount of sweet-savory "umami" to the dish. It's very easy to make Nouc Cham correctly but unfortunately it is hardly ever done right in the U.S. The sauces in Vietnamese restaurants always have watered-down fish sauce; they are not using palm sugar nor enough fresh lime juice and not the best fish sauce. Make this recipe just once to see what you have been missing.

1 ounce Thai red and green chiles (about 12 chiles)
1/2 cup lime juice
2 tablespoons palm sugar
4 teaspoons fish sauce (3 Crabs brand)
1/2 teaspoon minced garlic
1/4 teaspoon salt

Slice the Thai chiles in rings and place in a bowl with seeds. Add the lime juice, palm sugar, fish sauce, minced garlic, and salt. Yield 1 cup.

Serves 8
Heat level: **1 2 3 4 5 6 7** 8 9 10

Tip: *When you buy fish sauce, buy the most expensive and smallest bottle and the lightest color. After opening it, put it in the refrigerator and use it for only about two months maximum. Fish sauce gets stronger as it gets older and also gets less appealing. Using less of a bad fish sauce is not the right answer. A good amount of a superior, fresh fish sauce is the way to correct Asian seasoning. So date the bottle when you buy it, refrigerate after opening, and discard it after a couple of months.*

Piri Piri / AFRICA

Piri piri is a small flavor bomb! The favored chile of East Africa, it is also grown throughout Kenya, Tanzania, and South Africa and used to make the fiery hot salsas in bottles that usually accompany the inviting Creole, Indian, and African flavors of those regions. The piri piri is a domesticated cousin of a wild bird chile from the Americas that was transplanted by the Portuguese traders, or was traded across Africa in the sixteenth century on the spice routes. It grows profusely in tall plants that almost become bushes in this region. If unavailable, you can substitute fresh chile pequin or habaneros for piri piri.

1/4 cup rough chopped onion (about 1/2 small)
3 cloves garlic
1 teaspoon fresh grated ginger
3 tablespoons canola oil
2 tablespoons piri piri powder
1 teaspoon paprika, dulce
1/2 cup tomato juice
1 cup water
2 tablespoons tomato paste
1 1/2 teaspoons salt
1/4 cup white vinegar (Heinz brand)
2 tablespoons lemon juice
1 tablespoon Sriracha chile sauce

Place the onion, garlic, and ginger in a medium saucepan with the canola oil. Cook slowly over low heat for 7 minutes. Add the piri piri powder and paprika and cook for an additional 2 minutes. Add the tomato juice, water, tomato paste, and salt and cook for 5 minutes. Blend this mixture in a food processor then add the vinegar, lemon juice, and Sriracha sauce. Yield 2 cups.

Serves 8
Heat level: **1 2 3 4 5 6 7 8** 9 10

Ghost Chile (Naga Jolokia) / INDIA, BENGAL

When we say chiles are hot, this chile is like an atomic explosion! The ghost chile was "discovered" a few years ago in northeast India on the border of Bhutan in an area that is called Nagaland and was celebrated with much fanfare in the international press as the hottest chile in the world. Handle this chile with caution—it's the only one for which I recommend that you use a face mask to prevent breathing in the irritating volatile chile fumes. In fact, the Indian military is developing a hand grenade using this chile. We use the dried chiles in this recipe to add the necessary "fire" to the salsa.

1 medium onion, sliced in rings
2 cloves garlic
1 teaspoon candied ginger (1 small piece)
1 cup water
1/2 cup coconut vinegar or Heinz white vinegar
1 Naga Jolokia (ghost chile), stemmed
1 tablespoon jaggery sugar
1 pound tomatoes
2 teaspoons salt
3 tablespoons Panch Phoram Spice Mix

Place the onion in a saucepan with a lid. Add the garlic, candied ginger, water, coconut vinegar, ghost chile, and jaggery. Simmer for 10 minutes over low heat, covered. Remove the lid and reduce the liquid to 1/3 cup. Use caution when cooking uncovered as the fumes can rise and cause coughing and sneezing.

In a cast iron pan or comal heated to medium-high, roast the tomatoes for 8 to 10 minutes. In a blender, place the cooked ghost chile mixture, roasted tomatoes, salt, and Panch Phoram Spice Mix. Blend until smooth. Yield 2 1/3 cups.

Serves 8
Heat level: **1 2 3 4 5 6 7 8 9 10**

PANCH PHORAM SPICE MIX

1 tablespoon cumin seeds
1 tablespoon fennel seeds
1 tablespoon black mustard seeds
1 1/2 teaspoons Nigella seeds*
1 1/2 teaspoons fenugreek seeds

In a nonstick pan heated to medium-low, toast the cumin, fennel, mustard, Nigella, and fenugreek for 2 minutes, making sure not to burn. Grind the spices when cool; reserve.

8 Ripe and Fruity Salsas

Chipotle Peach / NEW MEXICO

This recipe uses mescal, to accentuate the smoky layers, as one of its essential ingredients. Mescal is the traditional liquor of Mexico; it's made from the hearts of agave plants, not just the Blue Azul Agave used in tequila. Del Maguey is the brand of the finest artisanal mescals made in the hilly areas outside of Oaxaca. Ron Cooper, a friend and inspirational modern artist from Taos, New Mexico, is the creator of this brand. Over a twenty year period, he single-handedly revived and saved this traditional way of making spirits in Mexico. These mescals are all made by hand by old mescaleros masters, who harvest wild agave plants and then roast them in earth ovens for three days. They then grind the smoky, roasted hearts in stone mills and ferment the juices, then distil the liquor over open pot-sill fires that absorb the smoky fumes from the wood fires. Del Maguey has won many gold medals in worldwide spirit competitions. If you enjoy a great smoky, peaty malt whisky, you will relish these mescals. Go to www.delmaguey.com to get more info and some cocktail inspirations.

1 pound 8 ounces yellow peaches
1/2 cup fine diced white onion
1 tablespoon white balsamic vinegar
1 tablespoon Chipotle Tabasco
1 tablespoon water
2 tablespoons mescal (Del Maguey Chichicapa brand)
2 tablespoons brown sugar
2 tablespoons sugar
2 tablespoons chipotle en adobo, deseeded, chopped fine (about 6)
2 tablespoons adobo sauce
1/8 teaspoon allspice
1/4 teaspoon Worcestershire (Lea & Perrins brand)
1 tablespoon mescal (Del Maguey Chichicapa brand)
1 teaspoon lemon juice

Bring a large pot of water to a boil. Prepare a large bowl of ice water. With a paring knife score an X on the bottom of the peaches and place, 3 at a time, in the boiling water for 15 to 20 seconds. Take peaches out of the boiling water and put into the ice water. Repeat with remaining peaches. Slip skins off peaches and discard; dice peaches in 3/8-inch cubes.

Place the onion in a large sauté pan with a lid. Add the white balsamic vinegar, Chipotle Tabasco, water, 2 tablespoons mescal, brown sugar, sugar, minced chipotles, adobo sauce, allspice, and Worcestershire. Cook over medium heat until all the liquid has evaporated. Pour mixture over diced peaches and add 1 tablespoon mescal and lemon juice. Yield 3 1/2 cups.

Serves 8
Heat level: **1 2 3 4 5** 6 7 8 9 10

Cherry Ancho Cocoa Nib / MEXICO

Cherries and chocolate. What a great classic combination of flavors! I wonder who thought of it first? Maybe some wild chocolatier back in Paris or Belgium in the 1700s who wanted to invent some new, outlandish flavors. This salsa re-creates the classic combination with a new Latin beat: it combines ripe, fragrant sweet cherries, earthy Ancho chiles to give it a dash of spice, and irresistibly captivating dark chocolate. This dish has its roots in pre-Columbian Mexico, where chocolate comes from the discovery of cacao in the New World. Cocoa nibs (crushed pieces from the roasted cocoa beans), rather than semi-sweet chocolate bits, are my preferred base for pure chocolate flavoring in most recipes, as they contain no sugars or off-putting flavors and have all the natural sweet and bitter notes of real dark chocolate. They are easy to find online or in any baking section of a good grocery store. Scharffen Berger Chocolate packages some excellent cocoa nibs.

1 ounce ancho chile powder or
  1 whole ancho, seeded
1 Arbol chile
1/2 cup cherries, pitted
1 cup cherry juice*
1 cup water
1/3 cup brown sugar
1/8 teaspoon allspice
1 tablespoon cocoa nibs
4 cups cherries, pitted, cut in half
2 tablespoons brown sugar
1/4 teaspoon smoked salt
2 tablespoons cocoa nibs

In a cast iron pan or comal heated to medium-low, toast the ancho and Arbol chile for 1 minute. Place in a medium saucepan. Add 1/2 cup cherries, cherry juice, water, 1/3 cup brown sugar, allspice, and 1 tablespoon cocoa nibs. Cook over medium heat for 10 minutes or until the liquid has reduced to 1 cup. Puree in a blender and strain into a mixing bowl.

In a nonstick pan, place 4 cups cherries, 2 tablespoons brown sugar, and smoked salt and sauté for 2 minutes to let the juice release. Remove the fruit and add to the puree. Reduce the liquid and then add to the fruit. Add 2 tablespoons cocoa nibs to finish. Yield 3 cups.

Serves 8
Heat level: **1 2** 3 4 5 6 7 8 9 10

**You can make your own cherry juice if you have a juicer. If you buy cherry juice, make sure it is pure cherry juice—not with water or sugar added and not reconstituted. Frozen cherries are available all year long and are great for this recipe.*

White Peach Habanero / GEORGIA, UNITED STATES

Many people think of the Southwest as colorful and possessing spectacular, epic scenery, but not necessarily as the home for great agriculture products—except chiles. But there is some great fruit grown here, and New Mexico has a short peach season in late summer that produces small but fabulous fruits. Peaches are grown in the Velarde Valley, north of Santa Fe along the Rio Grande on the road to Taos. The orchards are all irrigated by canals from the Rio Grande. This area was planted by Spanish settlers hundreds of years ago. They brought their beloved orchard fruits—apples, peaches, and pears—from their homeland to Mexico, and then from Mexico to New Mexico. This seed exchange was reinforced by the Spanish missions throughout the Southwest and California, which functioned as major agricultural stations for all the species of Old World plants brought to the New World. Even grapes thrived in New Mexico, and there is still a large wine industry in the center of the state. Look for great New Mexico wines, especially excellent sparkling wines that rival any other domestically produced labels.

1 habanero chile
2 tablespoons rice wine vinegar (Marukan brand)
1/4 cup agave syrup (Madhava brand)
About 1 1/2 pounds white peaches
1 teaspoon lime juice

In a cast iron pan or comal heated to medium-low, roast the habanero for 12 minutes. Mince and place in a medium saucepan with seeds. Add the rice wine vinegar and agave syrup. Cook for 4 minutes. Let cool in the saucepan.

In the meantime, prepare an ice bath. Prepare a large pot of boiling water. Cut an X on the bottom of the peaches then plunge them, 4 at a time, in the boiling water for 15 seconds. Remove and place in ice bath. Repeat with remaining peaches. Slip skins off and discard. Peel and dice the peaches, and place 3 cups in the saucepan with the chile mixture. Heat for 2 to 3 minutes, or until peaches are heated through. Turn off the heat and let cool completely. Add the lime juice. Yield 3 cups.

Serves 6–8
Heat level: **1 2 3 4 5 6** 7 8 9 10

Strawberry Fig Balsamic / ITALY

I had never had strawberries and vinegar together until I was dining in Venice at the end of a hot, steamy summer day. We were eating dinner, alfresco, in one of those charming secret gardens in the back of an old palazzo, where the ghosts of bygone eras seem to accompany you. A few twinkling candles, starched, pale, buttery linen tablecloths, and the eternal magic of Venice reappears. The set menu for the meal was a series of mini-surprises of exquisite local seafood, unassuming pastas, and local wines. And then came dessert, a treasure from the woods: warm, ripe, fragrant wild strawberries with a thin strip of twenty-year-old balsamic vinegar. A forceful mosaic of sweet, wild scents against the cultured, aged essence; it was nature at its purest and a highly evolved culinary aesthetic, all on one plate. Brilliant! This salsa captures those flavors and can be served with savory meat dishes like suckling pig, on top of vanilla gelato, or with a pound cake made from organic stone-ground polenta and olive oil.

2 tablespoons black peppercorns
1 teaspoon coriander seeds
2 Black Mission figs, dried
1/4 cup balsamic vinegar
2 tablespoons fig balsamic
1/2 cup water
1 pound strawberries
1 teaspoon lemon olive oil
1/8 teaspoon fresh ground black pepper

Crack the black peppercorns and coriander with the bottom of a small saucepan or in a mortar with a pestle. Chop the figs and place with the cracked spices together in a small saucepan. Add the balsamic vinegar, fig balsamic, and water. Cook until a thick syrup is achieved, about 7 to 10 minutes. Strain into a mixing bowl and cool.

Cut the strawberries into 3/8-inch cubes and add to the balsamic vinegar syrup. Add the lemon oil and, using a peppermill, grind 1/8 teaspoon fresh ground black pepper, or to taste, and add. Yield 2 cups.

Serves 6
Heat level: **1 2** 3 4 5 6 7 8 9 10

Tip: *When you buy Black Mission figs, make sure they are soft, as the old, dried-out ones lose some of their flavor along with their moisture. Also, use a very good black peppercorn like tellicherry; it has more perfume and less of the bitter, hot "pepper" notes.*

Korean Pear Barbeque / KOREA

Korean cuisine is another example of the universal practice of combining sweet and hot together. Koreans use Asian pear, sweet apples, or apple juice as the sweet note and a chile paste as the hot note; this is called "gochujang." The pungent Korean hot pepper paste is made from dried chile flakes; yeasted, glutinous rice; and fermented soybeans or fermented barley. All these ingredients are mashed together and, historically, left outside in stone jars for a number of years in the sun to age. The first record of this paste being made in Korea was in the early eighteenth century. The paste is now made commercially. It is the base flavor that colors other Korean sauces and stews, such as the famous Korean BBQ sauce. If you do any BBQ, you should get some gochujang to experiment with; it adds a complex savory note with lots of umami.

1 1/2 cups diced Asian pear
1 cup ginger ale, divided
4 cloves garlic
1/4 teaspoon salt
5 tablespoons Gochujang Korean hot pepper paste
1 tablespoon + 1 teaspoon Korean chile flakes
1 1/2 teaspoons Chipotle Tabasco
1 chipotle en adobo, seeded
1 tablespoon + 1 teaspoon Korean apple vinegar
1 tablespoon maple syrup (grade B, amber)
3 tablespoons + 1 teaspoon organic soy sauce
1 teaspoon lite soy
1 teaspoon sugar
2 teaspoons untoasted sesame oil

Peel and dice the pears. Place in a nonstick sauté pan and add 1/2 cup ginger ale and cook until the liquid has evaporated. Let cool. In a blender, add the pears, 1/2 cup ginger ale, garlic, salt, Gochujang pepper paste, Korean chile flakes, Chipotle Tabasco, chipotle, apple vinegar, maple syrup, soy, lite soy, sugar, and sesame oil. Blend until smooth. Yield 2 cups.

Serves 8
Heat level: **1 2 3 4 5 6** 7 8 9 10

Watermelon Barbeque / SOUTHERN STATES

Watermelon and BBQ are two great American traditions that express our ethos and our sense of community. They entreat us to be social and to share and create bonds that tie us together. Common foods that are classless and eaten in settings such as at picnic tables of wood sitting on shared benches bring us together. They are not reflective of hierarchical values or the economics of education or class but are foods that by their very nature are American and symbolize our culture. Watermelon is an icon that appears throughout folk paintings and commercial art. It's associated with a simpler, more innocent time—think of Huckleberry Finn—and the golden era when America was still becoming a great nation. This salsa is fun, tasty, colorful, and goes with anything you want to throw on the grill outside or cook on the beach.

2 cups canola oil
1/2 cup diced Fresno chiles (about 10)
1/2 cup diced red bell pepper
2 tablespoons diced red onion (1/8-inch pieces)
2 pounds seedless watermelon
1 tablespoon minced sweet hot habanero
3/4 teaspoon salt or hibiscus salt
3 tablespoons Cholula hot sauce
1 teaspoon sweet hot mustard (Inglehoffer brand)

In a deep-sided pan, heat the oil to 350 degrees F and oil roast the Fresnos and red bell pepper. Place in a plastic bag to steam. When cool, peel, deseed, and dice in 1/8-inch pieces. Place in a mixing bowl. Rinse the red onion in cold water. Drain and add to the bowl. Dice the watermelon in 1/8-inch pieces and add. Mince the pickled habanero and add to the bowl. Season with salt, Cholula hot sauce, and sweet mustard. Do not overmix this salsa as the watermelon will break down. Yield 4 cups.

Serves 8

Heat level: **1 2 3 4** 5 6 7 8 9 10

Tip: *Cholula hot sauce is the Mexican hot sauce with the picturesque country woman on the label and the small wooden top. Get the regular, not the newer flavors. It's a great standard and makes a good base. Make sure to use the Cholula brand of sweet mustard, and not some of the European sweet mustards that are a little bitter and with too much mustard seed flavor for this dish.*

Green Apple, Green Chile, Tomatillo / NEW MEXICO

Concentrated ripe apples, fire-roasted green chiles, cooling velvety tomatillos—all punctuated with herbaceous wild oregano; it's a medley of green harmonies. We make a strong flavor balance by combining fresh apples, dried apples, and apple cider. This is a perfect salsa for roasted pork loin or grilled pork chops, or as a side salsa for fried cinnamon-brined quail. Or try it on sautéed fresh pink shrimp on top of corn cakes.

1 cup diced fresh green apple
1/2 cup diced dried apple
1/2 cup apple cider
1 cup diced green chile
1 cup diced tomatillos
1/4 teaspoon oregano
1/2 teaspoon salt
1/2 teaspoon apple cider vinegar

Peel, core, and dice the green apple in 3/8-inch pieces. Dice the dried apple in 3/8-inch pieces. Place both apples in a saucepan and add the apple cider; cook over medium-low heat for 5 minutes or until liquid has evaporated.

Over an open flame, with a grill, fire roast the green chile, blistering the skin, then place in a plastic bag to steam. When cool, peel, deseed, and dice in 3/8-inch pieces.

Rinse the tomatillos 5 to 10 minutes, depending on the residue left on. The residue is what causes bitterness. Choose the same size tomatillos so that they cook evenly. Boil in salted water for 4 minutes. Shock in ice water to stop the cooking. When cool, core and dice in 3/8-inch pieces.

Toast the oregano in a nonstick sauté pan for 1 minute on medium-low heat.

To assemble the salsa, mix the prepared apples, prepared chile, and diced tomatillos. Add the oregano, salt, and apple cider vinegar. Yield 3 cups.

Serves 8
Heat level: **1 2 3 4** 5 6 7 8 9 10

Tip: *When shopping for apple cider, look for unfiltered, unpasteurized apple cider, even it's frozen; it makes a big difference. The next best option is unfiltered apple cider in a glass jug, and third best is frozen apple concentrate with nothing added. Do not use apple juice, as it's almost all water and corn syrup and very little apple essence.*

Aji Amarillo Passion Fruit / PERU

The aji family of chiles is a completely different family of chiles than the ones in North America and the Caribbean. They are available fresh (if you live in an area with a large South American population), frozen (from specialty food websites), or dried (whole or in powdered form). I use the frozen, whole, noncooked ones for this recipe. They have a punch to them. They're about 5 inches tall and 4 inches across, and bright yellow with jet black seeds inside. You cannot mistake them for a member of the Capsicum family. There are also the small bird hot chiles in this family, and the red rocoto chile that is used in all the famous Peruvian ceviches and tiraditos, which need fruit to balance them out. Here, the passion fruit purees, apple juice, and fruity habanero give the sauce a fresh brightness, sweetness, and exotic edge that goes perfectly with aji amarillo chiles. Use this salsa on grilled shrimp tacos, seafood dishes, raw fish crudos, or grilled chicken. Mix it in a tuna tartar or use it for a salad dressing.

1 pound yellow tomatoes, rough chopped
1 large yellow bell pepper, rough chopped
3 cloves garlic
1/2 cup rough chopped white onion (about 1/2 small)
6 aji amarillo chiles
1 habanero, seeded
1 teaspoon salt
2 tablespoons apple juice concentrate
1/3 cup diced passion fruit

Place the tomatoes, bell pepper, garlic, onion, aji amarillo chiles, habanero, salt, and apple juice concentrate in a large saucepan and cook, covered, over medium heat for 10 minutes. When cool, place in a blender and blend to a smooth consistency. Stir in the passion fruit. Yield 4 cups.

Serves 8
Heat level: **1 2 3 4 5** 6 7 8 9 10

Blood Orange, Ruby Red Grapefruit, Cascabel / YUCATÁN

This expressive bright red salsa has some underlying flavor complexities from the addition of the dark ruby red sweet-sour grapefruit to accompany the cascabel chile. The cascabel has one of the most complex fruit flavor profiles of all dried red chiles. It been compared to a classic Bordeaux with its dark, fruity overtones accompanied by perfumes of smoke, tobacco, and earthy accents. The ripe winter grapefruits have a wonderful sweet-sour citrus flavor that is underused in cooking. This is a great salsa with grilled fish with a rich flavor like salmon or scallops.

10 cascabel chiles
3 hibiscus flowers, dried
1 1/2 cups water
1/2 cup blood orange juice
1/4 cup ruby red grapefruit juice
1/2 teaspoon salt
1/2 cup thin sliced red onion
1/4 cup blood orange juice
3 tablespoons blood orange balsamic vinegar (Napa Valley)
1 teaspoon sugar
1/8 teaspoon tamarind paste (Neera brand)
3/4 cup blood orange segments (3/8-inch pieces)
3/4 cup ruby red grapefruit segments (3/8-inch pieces)

Seed the cascabels and place chiles in a small saucepan with a lid. Add the hibiscus flowers and water. Cook, covered, for 5 minutes, then remove lid and cook until all but 2 tablespoons of the liquid has evaporated. Let cool. Place the cascabels in a blender and puree with 1/2 cup blood orange juice and grapefruit juice. Season with salt and place in a mixing bowl.

Place the sliced red onion in a nonstick pan. Add 1/4 cup blood orange juice, balsamic vinegar, sugar, and tamarind paste. Cook until all the liquid has evaporated. Cool and add to the cascabel puree. Cut segments from the blood orange and grapefruit into 3/8-inch pieces and add to the cascabel puree. Yield 2 1/2 cups.

Serves 8
Heat level: **1 2 3 4** 5 6 7 8 9 10

Muhammara / SYRIA

In Istanbul around late October and early November, the city is invaded by pomegranates. The streets are lined with pomegranate juice stands where you can have a large glass freshly pressed in front of you by those old hand aluminum bar presses that you used to see in French zinc bars. The scarlet juice revives you—it's just the right balance of sweet and sour. Some of the stands pile the pomegranates up almost five feet high. The vendors cut them in half so you can see the fruits pregnant with huge, swollen, juicy seeds. There are thousands of pomegranates everywhere; you cannot escape them. They turn up in pastries, in salads, on top of yogurt and whole roasted fish . . . and then they disappear for another year.

4 red bell peppers
3 Fresno chiles
3/4 cup walnuts
1/2 teaspoon cumin seeds
1 cup diced white onion (1/4-inch pieces)
1/2 cup olive oil
Seeds from 1 pomegranate (about 1/2 cup)
1/4 cup olive oil
2 tablespoons breadcrumbs
4 tablespoons pomegranate molasses
1/2 teaspoon salt
1 pomegranate, juiced*

Preheat oven to 475 degrees F with the broiler unit turned on and place a rack just above the center of the oven. Roast the bell peppers and Fresnos for 12 minutes, turning to blister the skins. Place them in a plastic bag to steam. When cool, peel, and deseed. Reserve 1 bell pepper and dice the rest in 1/8-inch pieces. Reserve 1 Fresno and dice the rest in 1/8-inch pieces.

Turn the oven down to 300 degrees F and toast the walnuts and cumin seeds for 10 minutes; reserve. Sauté the onion in 1/2 cup olive oil until golden brown.

In a food processor, place the whole bell pepper, whole Fresno, walnuts, cumin, onion, 1/4 cup olive oil, breadcrumbs, pomegranate molasses, and salt. Puree. Fold in the diced bell pepper, diced Fresno, pomegranate seeds, and pomegranate juice. Yield 3 cups.

Serves 6
Heat level: **1 2 3** 4 5 6 7 8 9 10

**To juice a pomegranate, gently push the skin in to the center until it yields to the touch, being careful not to break the skin. Repeat by working around the fruit. When completely soft, use a paring knife and make an incision so that the juice can flow out.*

9 Hot and Sour Salsas

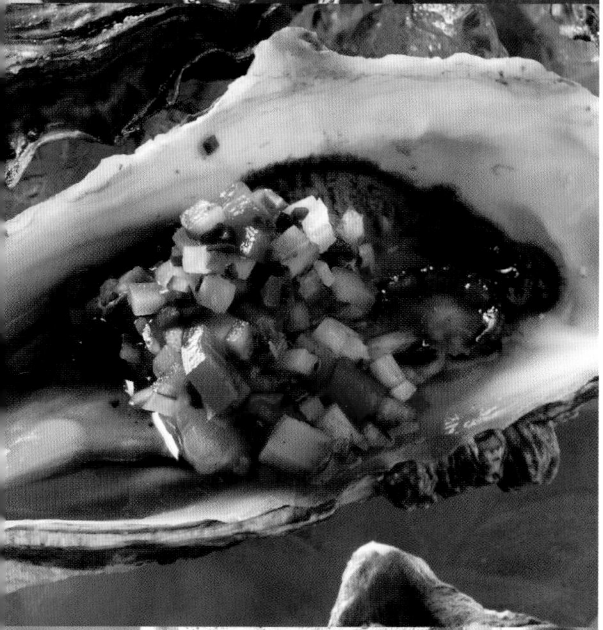

Lhasa Yellow Achar / TIBET

This is a long and complicated recipe, but think how hard (and expensive) it would be to go to Lhasa, in Tibet, find the ingredients and a recipe, have it translated from Tibetan into English, find a Tibetan pickle expert to show you how to make it, and then pack it up for travel and try to get through customs! So for your next Himalayan feast, or for any great Indian meal, try this salsa. And get a copy of my friend Naomi Duguid's book Mangoes and Curry Leaves: Culinary Travels Through the Great Subcontinent, *which includes amazing recipes and tales. I have participated in hands-on cooking classes with Naomi in northern Thailand, which proved to be some of the very best culinary learning experiences of my life. If you are interested in learning more about these wondrous cuisines from this incredible person, check out her website, www.hotsoursaltysweet.com, and her other fantastic books.*

PICKLED DAIKON RADISH

8 ounces daikon radish
1 shallot, sliced in thin strips
1 scallion, sliced in strips
1 tablespoon minced garlic
1 tablespoon salt
1 tablespoon jaggery sugar
1 teaspoon Szechuan peppercorns, ground
1 1/2 cups rice wine vinegar

Cut the radish on a mandoline in julienne pieces and place in a bowl. Add the shallots, scallions, and garlic to the bowl. Season with salt, jaggery, and Szechuan pepper. Heat the rice wine vinegar to a boil; pour over the radish mixture and cover. Let sit for 3 hours.

CHILE PASTE

2 tablespoons canola oil
1/4 Thailand red chile, dried, in flakes
1 teaspoon Szechuan peppercorns, ground
2 tablespoons minced shallot
1/2 cup water
1 tablespoon rice wine vinegar

Heat the oil in a sauté pan. Add the chile, Szechuan pepper, and shallots; cook until the shallots are translucent, about 3 minutes. Add the water and rice wine vinegar and cook for 3 more minutes.

SALSA

1 tablespoon fresh grated ginger
1 teaspoon fresh grated turmeric root*
2 tablespoons canola oil
1/4 cup minced shallots
1 teaspoon ground cumin
1/2 teaspoon coriander
1/8 teaspoon salt
2 teaspoons jaggery sugar
1 tablespoon Chile Paste (see page 164)
1 cup Pickled Daikon Radish, drained (see page 164)
3 pickled habanero sweet hots, sliced in strips
1/2 cup chopped cilantro

Grate the ginger and turmeric on a Microplane. Heat the oil in a nonstick sauté pan and cook the ginger, turmeric, shallots, cumin, and coriander for 3 minutes on medium-low. Add the salt, jaggery, Chile Paste, and Pickled Daikon Radish and heat through. Cool completely. Mix in the habanero sweet hots and cilantro. Yield 1 1/2 cups.

Serves 6
Heat level: **1 2 3 4 5 6** 7 8 9 10

Note: *The Chile Paste recipe and the Pickled Daikon Radish recipe can be used separately.*

**1/2 teaspoon turmeric powder may be substituted.*

Prik Nahm Pla / THAILAND

This is quintessential Thai salsa—to taste it is to hear the throbbing, blaring, clanking sounds of Bangkok, to feel a steamy sweat coming on, and to get the taste buds ready for a wild adventure! Thai food is the most bombastic cuisine in the world. It delights and scares the senses at the same time. It's filled with both sweet and hot flavors, the two qualities that make Thai food so delectable, and probably one of the reasons for its great popularity. Make sure to use a fresh fish sauce and Thai chiles, which have just the right amount of pop and not too much of a "green veggie" flavor tone. Besides, they are prettier.

6 Thai green chiles
6 Thai red chiles
1 medium carrot
1/4 cup + 2 tablespoons fish sauce (3 Crabs brand)
1/2 cup + 2 tablespoons lime juice
2 teaspoons sugar or palm sugar
Zest of 1 lime
2 teaspoons water

Slice the green and red Thai chiles in thin rings and place in a bowl. Cut the carrot on a Benriner mandoline in fine julienne; add to the chiles. Add the fish sauce, lime juice, sugar, lime zest, and water. Let sit for 15 minutes or up to 2 hours before serving. Yield 1 cup.

Serves 8
Heat level: **1 2 3 4 5 6 7 8** 9 10

Tip: *To use a microplane to zest a citrus fruit, put the fruit on the counter and very lightly rub the microplane over the surface. Don't push down on the plane or hold it too firmly in your hand, as you will scrape off some of the underlying pith, which is bitter. You only want the lightest scraping, not even zest—just lime or lemon dust. When you finish, there should be no white spots on the fruit indicating that you have scraped through the peel too far.*

Mango Pickle Fresh Chutney / INDIA

Grains of paradise, sometimes called melegueta peppers, are the seeds from a plant that is a member of the ginger/cardamom family. The taste is aromatic and pungent, with piney pepper tones at first, and eventually notes of camphor at the end. I first starting using this spice in my Moroccan cooking, where it adds a mysterious scent to tagines. I also use it in the intricate Moroccan spice blend Ras el Hanout. Besides its culinary use, the spice is used in artisanal gin recipes (which are making a big comeback, I am happy to see), and in the Scandinavian liquor aquavit. Marvelous with any lamb or eggplant dish, it pairs particularly well with cumin and cinnamon.

1/4 cup white vinegar (Heinz brand)
1 1/2 teaspoons sugar or jaggery*
1/2 teaspoon salt
1/4 teaspoon powdered fenugreek
1/8 teaspoon powdered cardamom (about 12 grains)
1/4 teaspoon powdered coriander
1/4 teaspoon grains of paradise, ground
2 teaspoons New Mexican red chile flakes
1/8 teaspoon dried lemon powder (Persian)
1 tablespoon lime juice
1/4 teaspoon ginger juice**
1 mango

Place the vinegar in a bowl. Place the sugar and salt in a mortar. Add the fenugreek, cardamom, coriander, grains of paradise, red chile flakes, and lemon powder and grind together. Add to the vinegar. Add the lime juice and ginger juice. Peel the mango, pit, and slice thinly on a Benriner mandoline. Place in a bowl and let marinate for 2 hours. Yield 1 1/2 cups.

Serves 6
Heat level: **1 2 3 4 5 6** 7 8 9 10

**Jaggery has a darker molasses note of flavor.*
***Grate fresh ginger and then squeeze the juice.*

Kim Chee Ham Hock / KOREA

The idea of kim chee and ham hock together is not so crazy; think of a kosher dill pickle with a pastrami sandwich, or sweet pickles with Texas BBQ, or a slice of pickle on a hamburger. The combination of a pickle and a richly flavored meat or cured meat is universal. This is not an original Korean salsa; it was formed from two favorite foods for Koreans and two of my favorite foods: pork and kim chee. I have had a lifelong friendship with smoked ham hocks. They were the basis of my grandmother's great split yellow pea soup, a classic winter Arcadian dish in Canada. And what does Nova Scotia have to do with Korea? They both have long, hard, bitterly cold winters. Many delicious, rich foods that warm the belly and soul come from areas where there is not a lot of sunshine. Korean cuisine uses many chile powders, sweet chiles, fermented chiles, hot chiles, and smoky chile sauces. I only wish we'd had more of those elements in my grandmother's food; they would have made for interesting family recipes!

1 cup diced Bosc pear
1 smoked ham hock
1/4 cup apple juice concentrate (Tree Top brand)
1 teaspoon Korean red miso chile paste
1 cup water
2 teaspoons sesame chile oil
5 teaspoons Korean chile flakes
6 shisito chile peppers
1/3 cup sliced green onion (1/2-inch pieces)
1 1/2 cups prepared kim chee
2 tablespoons sesame seeds, toasted

Peel the pear and cut in 1/4-inch pieces. Place the ham hock, apple juice concentrate, diced pear, miso paste, and water in a saucepan with a lid and steam ham hock slowly for 20 minutes. Let cool. Pick the meat from the ham hock and dice in 1/3-inch pieces. Place all the liquid and pears from the pan in a mixing bowl and add the ham meat.

In a sauté pan, place the sesame oil, chile flakes, shisito peppers, and green onion and cook until the skins blister on the peppers. Cool, and then cut the peppers in rings. Using a rubber spatula, remove the chile flakes, green onion, and oil from the pan. Add to the ham meat. Cut the prepared kim chee in 1/4-inch pieces and add to the ham meat. Sprinkle with sesame seeds and mix well. Yield 3 cups.

Serves 8
Heat level: **1 2 3 4 5** 6 7 8 9 10

Buffalo Hot Wing Salsa / BUFFALO, UNITED STATES

What can I say about this salsa, except that it is the best buffalo hot wing salsa in the world! I dare you to come up with a better recipe. The bottled versions are anemic and boring compared to this. They are just hot, or just hot and vinegary without great flavor. A great wing deserves a great salsa to go with it. This salsa has all the classic flavor accents—rich and buttery, fiery and smoky, garlicky and spicy, the right amount of pickle, and fresh, sharp vinegar and pepper—all blended perfectly. I usually never say a recipe is perfect. But this is the perfect hot wing salsa. Try it on grilled shrimp, as a basting sauce for lobster tails, or added to tomato juice for Bloody Marys.

3 tablespoons butter
1 clove garlic
2 tablespoons cayenne pepper
1 tablespoon ground pequin chile
12 ounces spicy tomato juice
1/4 cup pickled red jalapeño, pureed (La Costeña)
1 tablespoon Sriracha sauce
1/2 teaspoon salt
3/4 teaspoon smoked salt
3 tablespoons ketchup
1 tablespoon tomato paste (Whole Foods 365 brand)
3 tablespoons Tabasco
1/4 cup Habanero Tabasco
1/4 cup white vinegar (Heinz brand)
1/8 teaspoon black pepper
1/4 teaspoon celery seed

Heat the butter and garlic in a medium saucepan. Let the butter brown on low temperature. Add the cayenne and pequin chile and let cook for 30 seconds. Add the spicy tomato juice. Remove any carrots that are in the pickled red jalapeño. Puree the pickled red jalapeños with juice in a food processor and add to the salsa. Add the Sriracha, salt, smoked salt, ketchup, tomato paste, Tabasco, Habanero Tabasco, white vinegar, black pepper, and celery seed and bring to a boil. Puree in a blender and strain. Yield 2 cups.

Serves 12
Heat level: **1 2 3 4 5 6 7 8 9** 10

Bloody Maria / MEXICO

This fresh Latin rendition of the classic Bloody Mary has quite a bit more bite than normal—just what you need to have a little more zing in your step after a long night of reveling! The interior celery stems and leaves are a softer vegetable flavor that have more of an aromatic quality and less of a grassy, stemmy feel. Try this wonderful salsa on raw oysters for brunch.

1 pound Roma tomatoes
3 tablespoons grated horseradish
2 serrano chiles
3 tablespoons celery leaves
1 tablespoon medium chopped cilantro leaves
4 ounces V8 spicy tomato juice
1 1/4 teaspoons salt
1/2 teaspoon fructose
3/4 teaspoon Worcestershire (Crosse and Blackwell brand)
1 teaspoon Tabasco
1/4 teaspoon fresh cracked black pepper
1 tablespoon lime juice
2 teaspoons lemon oil
1 shot Anejo tequila

Dice the tomatoes in 3/8-inch pieces and place in a mixing bowl. Peel and grate the horseradish on a Microplane and add to the bowl. Mince the serranos and add with seeds. Use the interior of the celery and dice mostly the leaves into 1/8-inch dice. Add to the bowl. Add the cilantro leaves. Add the V8 juice, salt, fructose, Worcestershire, Tabasco, black pepper, lime juice, lemon oil, and tequila. Yield 2 cups.

Serves 6
Heat level: **1 2 3 4 5 6 7** 8 9 10

Mosaic Mignonette / SOUTHERN FRANCE

The word mignonette *is derived from the French word* mignon, *which means "dainty," "tiny," or "delicate."* Mignonette *can mean coarse ground pepper or refer to the classic oyster preparation, which includes vinegar, coarse black pepper (mignonette), and finely diced shallots. This is my version of mignonette for oysters that includes more color, more spice, and, of course, chiles! The salsa can be used for any cold raw seafood where you would normally use vinegar or mignonette sauce. When the preparation is very simple like this one, pay special attention to the quality of the ingredients. For example, use real tellicherry whole black peppercorns and high-quality imported vinegars. It would be a shame to use anything but the best on pristine oysters and clams, which do not come cheap.*

3 tablespoons champagne vinegar
1 tablespoon rice wine vinegar (Marukan brand)
1 tablespoon fine diced shallots
2 tablespoons fine diced Persian cucumber
1/4 cured lemon
1 pickled Fresno chile
1 teaspoon sliced chives
3/8 teaspoon Fleur de Sel
1/4 teaspoon medium ground tellicherry black pepper

Place the champagne vinegar in a bowl and add the rice wine vinegar. Dice the shallots with a sharp knife and add to the vinegar. On a Benriner mandoline, cut the outer skin off the cucumber, slicing 2 layers, and then turn the cucumber a quarter turn and make 2 more slices. Continue until you reach the starting point. You should end with a rectangle. Dice 2 tablespoons and add to the vinegar.

Remove the pith from the cured lemon and dice fine; add. Remove the seeds from the pickled Fresno and dice fine. Add to the vinegar. Slice the chives with a very sharp knife into fine rings. Never push the knife into the chives as this will just make juice; cut with a pulling motion across. A razor blade may be used. Add the chives, Fleur de Sel, and fresh ground pepper. Yield 1 cup.

Serves 6
Heat level: **1 2 3** 4 5 6 7 8 9 10

Pickled Jalapeño Fresno / MEXICO

Throughout Mexico, bowls of pickled jalapeños with carrots and onions are a common condiment in taco stands, cevicherias, and tortas shops. The customers dip into these bowls for a high-octane chile rush or cooling, cleansing vinegar to balance the meaty fried carnitas, smoky barbacoa tacos, and buttery cheese quesadillas. The pickling tradition was introduced into Mexican cuisine by the Spanish, who have an extensive tradition of pickled, or escabeches, *dishes. Many of these dishes were in turn learned from the Moors, who occupied Spain for more than 700 years and left a lasting imprint on Spanish cuisine. This recipe uses both jalapeños and their cousin, the red Fresno chile, to provide more color and fire to the regular recipe. I always have a jar of Pickled Jalapeño Fresno in the fridge, and use them as an accent in many preparations. They last for months, so make a couple of batches and give them as gifts.*

8 ounces whole jalapeño chiles
8 ounces whole Fresno chiles
2 carrots
12 white boiling onions
2 cloves garlic
1/4 cured lemon
2 teaspoons salt
1 sprig thyme
6 sprigs cilantro
1 teaspoon coriander seeds
2 teaspoons dried oregano
2 bay leaves
1 tablespoon olive oil
3 1/2 cups white vinegar (Heinz brand)

Wash the two types of chiles in water thoroughly. Pierce each chile with a small knife. Place in a bowl. Peel the carrots and cut into 3/8-inch coins. Place in the bowl. Peel the boiling onions and remove the cores; add to the bowl. Peel the garlic and cut in halves. Place in the bowl.

In an 8-cup Mason jar, place the cured lemon, salt, thyme, cilantro, coriander, oregano, bay leaves, and olive oil. Mix the ingredients in the bowl and add to the Mason jar, trying to get an even mix of chiles and aromatics. Pour in the vinegar to the very top of the jar. Seal with a lid with a rubber gasket. Place in a steamer for 30 minutes. Cool at room temperature. Yield 8 cups.

Serves 12
Heat level: **1 2 3 4 5 6 7 8** 9 10

Remoulade / FRANCE

The taste design of the original remoulade is to use a rich egg yolk and olive oil base and infuse it with different and interesting savory flavors such as fresh herbs, citrus perfumes, pickled accents, and anchovy essence. Each ingredient is distinct and powerful and creates an intricate, explosive harmony of flavors, textures, and colors. You can't achieve all that from a bottled product made in a factory that sits on a shelf for a year. This recipe is straightforward and has no difficult steps, and if you want to use a very good commercial mayonnaise as a base it will go really quickly. Make sure that it's a real mayonnaise containing egg yolks, spices, and good olive or vegetable oil, not some emulsified miracle of a factory lab.

1 egg yolk, room temperature
1/2 teaspoon Fleur de Sel, ground fine
1 1/2 teaspoons Dijon mustard
1 teaspoon vinegar, from bottled cornichons
1 teaspoon lemon juice
1 cup grapeseed oil
1 1/2 teaspoons minced cured lemon, pith removed
1/2 teaspoon New Mexico dried red chile powder
1 teaspoon fine chopped tarragon
1 teaspoon fine chopped chervil
1 teaspoon fine chopped parsley
1 tablespoon finely sliced chives
6 cornichon pickles, minced

Place the egg yolk in a clean bowl. Place the bowl on a kitchen towel so that it does not move around as you mix in the oil. Season with Fleur de Sel, Dijon mustard, vinegar, and lemon juice.

Measure the oil and set it next to the bowl. With a flexible wire whisk, beat the egg yolk until it becomes whitened. Use a tablespoon of oil to start and mix it in until you can no longer see any oil. Add another tablespoon of oil, and repeat. Continue until about half the oil has been added, whisking constantly. If the mayonnaise is too thick, add a tablespoon of water. Continue to add the oil until the mayonnaise is complete. Add the cured lemon, red chile powder, tarragon, chervil, parsley, chives, and cornichons. Yield 1 1/2 cups.

Serves 6
Heat level: **1** 2 3 4 5 6 7 8 9 10

Tip: *Chervil may be hard to find, but seek it out and make it your culinary friend. It has a beguiling perfume and taste of light anise and fennel or parsley, but different. It's easy to grow in a kitchen herb garden. Always use fresh chervil; the dried variety is useless.*

Carrot Habanero / MEXICO

In this recipe I add carrot juice to intensify the carrot flavor and to get a brighter color and thicker consistency. This technique of adding vegetable or fruit juices, or frozen concentrates or dried pastes from tomatoes or dried fruits, gives the salsa that extra flavor intensity that I favor in my food. A lot of times with hot or spicy salsas, I find that the chiles or spices have overwhelmed the original flavors of the fruits or vegetables, so adding juices brings the recipe into a more pleasing balance and you get a much more interesting composition of flavors. Also, don't be such a purist as to work with only fresh ingredients all the time—drying, curing, or pickling not only intensifies natural flavors, but also develops more complex flavors.

1 cup grated carrots
4 tablespoons thin sliced fennel
3 habaneros, sliced in half, stems removed*
2 cloves garlic
2 teaspoons salt
1 cup white vinegar (Heinz brand)**
1/2 cup store-bought carrot juice
1/2 cup water***
2 tablespoons seasoned rice wine vinegar, red pepper (Nakano brand)
1 tablespoon picillo peppers or roasted bell pepper (see page 183)
2 teaspoons olive oil
1 tablespoon silver tequila

Place the carrots in a saucepan. Add the fennel and habaneros. Peel and cut the garlic in halves and add to the carrots. Add the salt, vinegar, carrot juice, and water. Cover and cook for 15 minutes on a low simmer. Cool completely. When cool, place in a blender and puree. Add the rice wine vinegar, picillo peppers, olive oil, and tequila. This salsa can be thinned by adding fresh carrot juice. Yield 1 3/4 cups.

Serves 8
Heat level: **1 2 3 4 5 6 7 8** 9 10

Tip: *Only buy fresh small- to medium-sized carrots with their tops still on, not baby carrots (which do not have enough flavor). The carrot tops can be used as the base. Larger carrots are woody and not as sweet; they can also be a little bitter. Prepeeled carrots are not fresh.*

**Remove seeds if a less spicy version is desired.*

***Acid level should be 6 percent.*

****Use carrot juice instead of water for a sweeter salsa.*

Salsa de Bruja / MEXICO

A bewitching salsa if there ever was one! With great colors and amazing flavors, it changes ordinary fried food into something special and magical. The name of this salsa means "salsa of the witch." The name probably comes from the strange variety of spices contained in the salsa, much like the folk healing potions available from the many curadors *you see in the markets of Mexico selling bundles of strange spices and herbs for whatever ails you. The best salsas de bruja are made inhouse and served in glass bottles on the tables of seafood restaurants. They're perfect for grilled or fried shrimp or fish, or really any fried item, including french fries. Use it much like you would add vinegar to fried fish and chips in England. The vinegar cuts the oiliness of the frying. This salsa has some great flavors besides the vinegar. Try to make it as colorful and strange as possible; it gets a stronger response from your guests if you tell them it's a secret recipe! Old tequila bottles are perfect containers, and it's important to place the salsa in the sun to improve the extraction of the flavors. If you cannot find chile tepin, use another very small, dried, hot chile.*

4 dried habanero chiles
2 fresh habanero chiles
2 fresh red serrano chiles
2 cups apple cider vinegar, unpasteurized (Spectrum brand)
1 teaspoon black pepper
1 teaspoon allspice
2 sun-dried tomatoes
20 tepin chiles, toasted
2 teaspoons Mexican oregano
2 fresh bay leaves
1 fresh thyme sprig

Slice the stems off the dried habaneros and discard. Slit the fresh habaneros lengthwise 4 times each. Slit the fresh serranos lengthwise 4 times each.

In a glass jar or bottle, add the vinegar, black pepper, allspice, sun-dried tomatoes, dried habaneros, fresh habaneros, serranos, tepin chiles, Mexican oregano, bay leaves, and thyme. Cover and place in the sun for 2 days. Yield 2 cups.

Serves 8
Heat level: **1 2 3 4 5 6** 7 8 9 10

10 Basic Recipes

Roasting Fresh Chiles and Bell Peppers

Roasting chiles and bell peppers brings out their natural sweetness, enhances their complex flavors, and adds a robust, smoky element. This technique also helps in peeling off the tough skin, which can be bitter. When it is important to retain the color, rather than creating the element of smoke in chiles or bell peppers, oil roasting is preferable. After you have handled chiles, do not touch your face or eyes until you have washed your hands thoroughly or you can burn yourself. Wearing rubber gloves is recommended. The work area in which you have placed the chiles needs to be thoroughly cleaned when you are finished.

FIRE ROASTING

Place the chiles or bell peppers over an open flame covered with a grill grate, on a barbeque grill, or under a broiler. You can also use a hand-held butane torch. Blister and blacken the skins all over, being careful not to burn the flesh. Transfer chiles or peppers to a bowl and cover with plastic wrap, or transfer to a plastic bag, and let steam for 15 to 20 minutes. When chiles are cool enough to handle, remove the skins with your fingers or with the tip of a small knife. Remove the seeds and internal ribs if the recipe calls for it. Removing the seeds and membrane will diminish the heat of the chiles. Never wash the chiles under water, as this will remove the natural oils and capsicum.

OIL ROASTING

Heat 1 cup canola oil to 350 degrees F in a deep-sided pan. Just before the oil smokes, place the chiles or bell peppers in the pan and blister the skin for 1 minute per side until all the skin has blistered. Use caution as the oil and water from the chiles will splatter. The use of a frying screen is recommended. Place the chiles or bell peppers in a bowl and cover with plastic wrap, or place in a plastic bag, and let steam for 15 to 20 minutes. When the chiles are cool enough to handle, remove the skins with your fingers or with the tip of a small knife. Remove the seeds and membrane if the recipe calls for it.

DRY ROASTING

In a heavy bottomed cast iron pan or comal heated to medium, place the chiles or peppers and roast for 8 to 12 minutes, depending on the size. This method works well for smaller chiles and jalapeños with thinner skins.

Roasting and Blackening Tomatoes

Roasting and blackening tomatoes gives them a more rustic, robust, complex flavor. It also concentrates the sugars and reduces water content. Another result of roasting and blackening is that it helps in the preservation of a salsa if the salsa is not consumed all in one day. All tomato varieties have salsas that are tailor-made for them. Smaller tomatoes have a more concentrated umami flavor. When choosing tomatoes, look for uniform size and the darkest color possible on the vine. Consider using heirloom and local varieties whenever possible.

ROASTING

Place the tomatoes in a heavy bottom cast iron pan or comal heated to medium-low. When the tomatoes start browning, not blackening, turn often. This takes about 8 minutes for cherry tomatoes, 10 to 12 minutes for Early Girls, 12 to 14 minutes for roma tomatoes, and 14 to 16 minutes for larger tomatoes. This can also be done in the oven with a broiler (with the rack centered), or in an oven set to 425 degrees F, using the same approximate times.

BLACKENING

In a heavy bottom cast iron pan or comal heated to medium-high, place tomatoes in the pan and don't move them. Make sure to blacken the skins well. This takes about 4 minutes per side for cherry tomatoes, for a total of about 8 minutes. For Early Girls 8 to 10 minutes, 10 to 12 minutes for roma tomatoes, and for larger tomatoes 12 to 14 minutes.

FIRE ROASTING

Place tomatoes over an open flame set to medium, covered with a grill grate, and turn every minute or until the skin blisters, being careful not to burn fully. Do not over-blacken or a bitter taste will result. A handheld butane torch can also be used.

OVEN DRYING

To oven dry tomatoes, preheat an oven to 225 degrees F. Prepare a large pot of boiling water. Prepare a large ice bath. Score the bottom of roma tomatoes and core, then plunge in boiling water for 10 to 15 seconds; place in the ice water. Peel the skins and discard, and cut the Romas lengthwise in half, place in a bowl, and season with salt and fructose and desired flavorings, such as garlic, herbs, spices, and chile powders. Place tomatoes cut side down on a baking sheet covered with Silpat or sprayed with nonstick cooking spray and oven dry for 3 hours. If not using immediately, tomatoes can be stored in a jar, covered with olive oil.

Roasting Garlic

DRY ROASTING

Place unpeeled garlic cloves in a heavy bottom cast iron pan and dry roast the garlic over medium-low heat for 15 to 20 minutes, turning occasionally until the garlic softens and browns on the outside. When roasted, you should be able to squeeze the garlic out of the peel. Roasted garlic is mellower, sweeter, and more subtle in flavor than raw garlic. Raw garlic flavors can dominate other ingredients and over a small time period will take over a whole dish. Blanching raw garlic in boiling salted water is recommended if you want a less aggressive garlic flavor.

OVEN ROASTING

To oven roast the garlic, set the temperature to 350 degrees F and place the garlic in a heavy bottom sauté pan. Bake, uncovered, for 25 to 30 minutes.

OIL ROASTING

To oil roast the garlic, place 3/4 cup oil in a small pan with a lid and add about 20 peeled whole garlic cloves. Season with salt and place in a preheated oven set to 350 degrees F; roast for 30 to 40 minutes. You can make herb-roasted garlic by adding fresh herbs to flavor the oil.

SMOKING

Fill the bottom of a stovetop smoker with apple wood chips, cover with second internal pan, and set a wire rack on top of that pan. Cut the top off the whole garlic, just enough to expose the inside, cutting about 1/8 inch into the garlic cloves. Place the garlic in the stovetop smoker and put on the stove. Heat the gas flame to high and ignite the wood chips for 2 to 3 minutes, then turn to low to keep the smoke going; continue for 20 minutes more. Transfer the smoker to a preheated oven set to 400 degree F and cook an additional 20 minutes.

Roasting Onions and Shallots

WHOLE ROASTED ONIONS

Preheat oven to 450 degrees F. Place medium whole sweet variety onions with the root side up in a large, heavy bottom sauté pan lined with parchment paper (this will help during cleanup), and bake for 2 hours. The outside onion skin will burn. Let the onions cook the full 2 hours, then let cool completely. Peel away the skin and use the inner parts. These onions get better with time when they are left to absorb the flavor of the sweeter roasted outer layer.

BLACKENED ONIONS

Preheat a heavy bottom cast iron pan to medium-low. Cut onions on the equator, slicing into 1/3-inch rings, and place these circles directly on the pan. Don't move the onions; they need to crust. After about 6 minutes, flip the onions over and roast the other side for an additional 6 minutes. The volume loss is about half. It is helpful to roast extra onions; they always come in handy.

ROASTED SHALLOTS

Preheat oven to 350 degrees F. Peel shallots and cut in half; season with salt. Lightly oil a sheet pan and lay shallots on pan cut side down. Roast for 35 to 40 minutes, let cool, mince, or used as called for in recipe.

FRIED SHALLOTS

Double the amount of shallots required for any recipe before frying. Preheat 3/4 cup oil to 350 degrees F. Slice 1 1/2 cups shallots lengthwise (for small strips). Fry for about 4 to 5 minutes, turning often. When golden brown, remove to a paper towel to drain. Yield 3/4 cup.

Toasting and Hydrating Dried Chiles and Seeds

Toasting chiles activates the oils in the skins, giving added flavor. The seeds also can be toasted to add a nuttiness and heat to certain salsas. It also adds a smoky element. Toasting chiles can aid in the removal of seeds if chiles are very dry.

To toast seeds, preheat a cast iron pan to low heat or heat an oven to 250 degrees F. Stem chile and remove as many seeds as possible, add the seeds to the pan, and shake continuously for about 1 1/2 minutes (double the time if cooking in an oven). The seeds will continue to cook so it is important to transfer them from the hot pan to a plate when done toasting. When cool, use a spice mill to grind seeds.

To toast chiles, place them in a single layer in the cast iron pan and toast for 2 minutes per side, making sure not to overtoast or a bitter taste may result. Remove and place in a bowl with enough hot water to cover. Put a plate on top to keep the chiles under water for 20 minutes. Taste the water to see if it has a bitter taste; if so, drain chiles and use fresh water or some portion of the hydrating liquid. This is a taste judgment, but mostly the hydrating water is recommended. Use chiles as prescribed in recipe.

Roasting Corn

Place a wide, shallow bowl in front of you and place the corncob standing up in the bowl. Cut the corn kernels from the cob with a sharp chef's knife, letting the kernels fall in the bowl. Try not to cut into the cob, but try to cut 1/3 of the way into the kernels; the closer the cut is to the cob the more fibrous the end product will become. The remaining corn milk can be scraped into another bowl with the back of a knife, seasoned, and cooked.

Place the corn kernels in single layers in a hot pan, and after 1 minute start to shake the pan. Shake again after 1 more minute and the corn should start to pop. Repeat a third and fourth time for a total of 4 minutes.

Cured Lemons

8 Meyer lemons
1/2 cup kosher salt
4 Arbol chiles, dried
2 bay leaves
1 cinnamon stick
1 bunch fresh thyme
1/2 cup lemon juice

Prepare a large canning jar. Cut the lemons into quarters and place one layer on the bottom of the jar; sprinkle with some of the salt and the chiles. Add a second layer of lemons, salt, and the bay leaves. Continue with more lemons, salt, and cinnamon stick. Finish with the last layer of lemons and thyme. Top off the jar with lemon juice and remaining salt. Seal with a lid and let sit out at room temperature for 3 weeks. Refrigerate for up to 6 months

Sources

Amigo Foods
800-627-2544
www.amigofoods.com
Rocoto chile peppers, South American products

Bueno Foods
2001 4th Street SW
Albuquerque, New Mexico 87102
800-95CHILE (800-952-4453)
505-243-2722
www.buenofoods.com
Fresh and frozen Hatch green chiles

The Chile Guy
168 East Calle Don Francisco
Bernalillo, New Mexico 87004
800-869-9218
505-867-4251
www.thechileguy.com
Largest assortment and best quality of dried chiles from Mexico and New Mexico, organic ancho chile powder, dried green Hatch chile, Mexican oregano, chile caribe, chipotle chiles, New Mexican chile pods, cascabels, chile pasilla, pasilla de Oaxaca

The Chile Shop
109 East Water Street
Santa Fe, New Mexico 87501
505-983-6080

Kalustyan's
123 Lexington Avenue
New York, New York 10016
800-352-3451 (toll free, only in the US)
212-685-3451 (phone)
212-683-8458 (fax)
www.kalustyans.com
All assorted dried chiles, yogurt sun-dried chiles, aleppo chiles, dried spices, aji amarillo, aji panca, ghost chiles

La Tienda
1325 Jamestown Road
Williamsburg, VA 23185
800-710-4304
www.tienda.com
Fresh pimentos de padron, serrano ham

Los Chileros
PO Box 6215
Santa Fe, New Mexico 87502
888-EAT-CHILE (toll free)
505-768-1100 (phone)
505-242-7513 (fax)
www.loschileros.com
Good selection of high-quality chiles and organic New Mexican chile powders

SaltWorks
15000 Wood-Red Road NE
Building B-900
Woodinville, WA 98072
800-353-7258
Smoked salt, Fleur de Sel

Spanish Table
109 N. Guadalupe Street
Santa Fe, New Mexico 87501
505-986-0243
www.spanishtable.com
Smoked salt, chorizo, Roland brand sun-dried tomatoes, anchovies, sherry vinegar, balsamic vinegar, saffron, pine nuts, Marcona almonds, Spanish olive oil, and smoked, dulce, and bittersweet paprika

Uwajimaya
600 5th Avenue South
Seattle, WA 98104
206-624-6248
800-889-1928
www.uwajimaya.com
Fresh Asian produce, soy sauces, dried scallops, dried shrimp, assorted Asian dry goods

Index

Metric Conversion Chart

Volume Measurements		Weight Measurements		Temperature Conversion	
U.S.	Metric	U.S.	Metric	Fahrenheit	Celsius
1 teaspoon	5 ml	1/2 ounce	15 g	250	120
1 tablespoon	15 ml	1 ounce	30 g	300	150
1/4 cup	60 ml	3 ounces	90 g	325	160
1/3 cup	75 ml	4 ounces	115 g	350	180
1/2 cup	125 ml	8 ounces	225 g	375	190
2/3 cup	150 ml	12 ounces	350 g	400	200
3/4 cup	175 ml	1 pound	450 g	425	220
1 cup	250 ml	2 1/4 pounds	1 kg	450	230